IMPORTANT INFORMATION

This book provides general information regarding psychological and mental wellbeing, and does not take account of individual circumstances. This book is not in any way a substitute for mental health treatment or medical advice. Always consult with a mental health professional or a qualified medical practitioner to address your or your kids' specific needs. The author and the publisher do not accept any liability for any injury, loss, or damage that may arise from reliance on the information contained in this book.

The names and personal details of clients have been changed to protect their privacy.

PHOENIX TIGER PRESS

Phoenix Tiger Press
Text © Belinda Siew Luan Khong 2025
Illustrations © Pip Tweed 2025
The author has asserted her moral rights
Order books at belindakhong.com
Book Design by letterdot.com.au
Printed by IngramSpark

Library of Congress Cataloging-in-Publication Data
Names: Khong, Belinda Siew Luan, author / Pip Tweed, illustrator
Title: Raising Spring Kids: A Psychologist's Guide to Nurturing Mindful Kids
by Belinda Siew Luan Khong; illustrated by Pip Tweed
Description: North Turramurra, Australia: Phoenix Tiger Press, 2025 / Summary: Raising Spring Kids:
A Psychologist's Guide to Nurturing Mindful Kids – Provided by publisher.
ISBN: 979-8-9868491-6-4 (Hardcover)
ISBN: 979-8-9868491-7-1 (Paperback)
Subjects: LCSH: Chinese New Year/Snake/Mental health/Children's Poetry/Mindfulness (Psychology)
Parenting/Psychosocial/Well-being/Gratitude/Resilience/Compassion/Emotional intelligence/Creativity
Manufactured in the United States of America

Raising Spring Kids

A Psychologist's Guide to Nurturing Mindful Kids

WITH A LITTLE HELP FROM OUR ANIMAL FRIENDS!

SPIRITUAL POSITIVE RESILIENT IMAGINATIVE NIMBLE GRATEFUL

Belinda Siew Luan Khong, PhD

Illustrated by **Pip Tweed**

CONTENTS

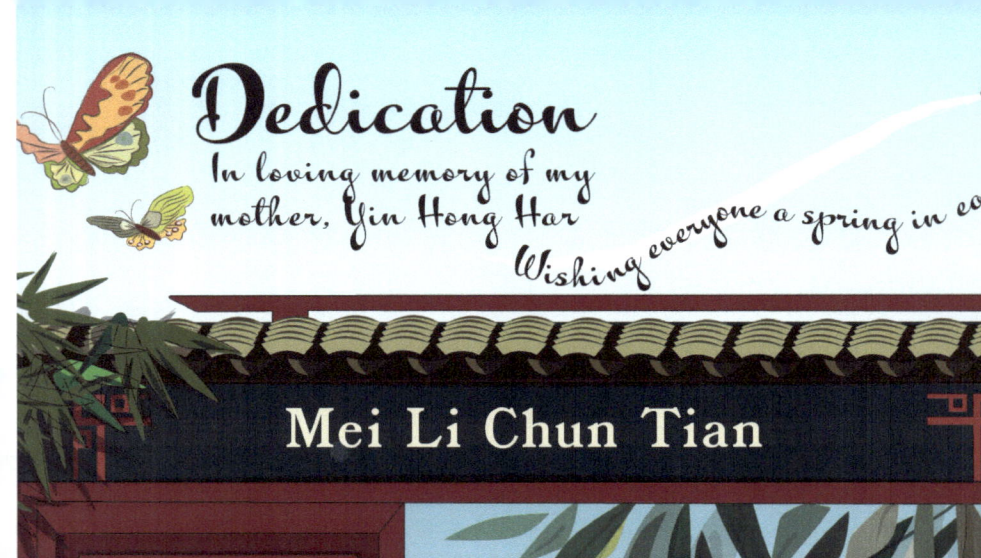

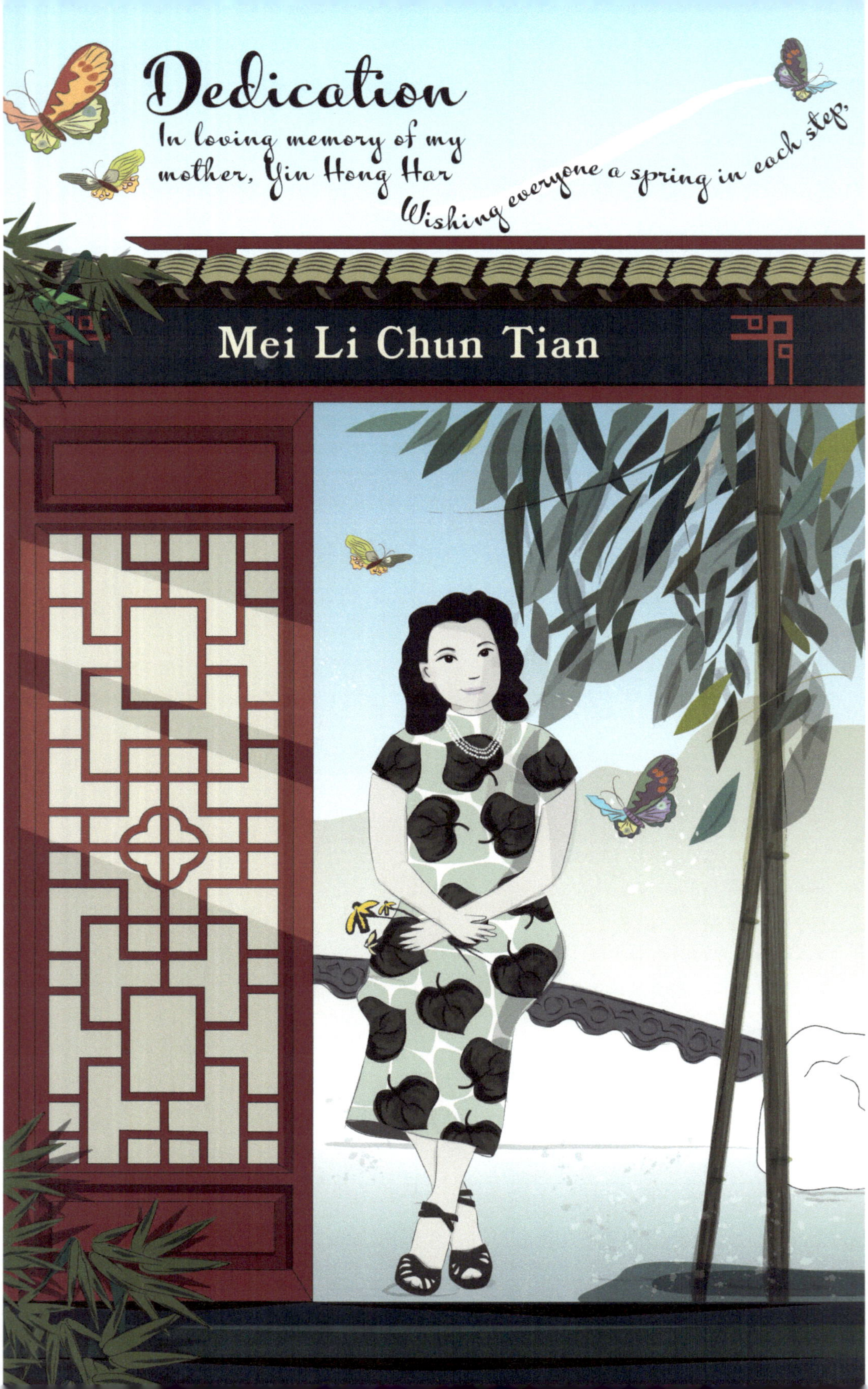
Dedication
In loving memory of my mother, Yin Hong Har
Wishing everyone a spring in each step,
Mei Li Chun Tian

And in every day of their lives,

With renewal, hope and growth.

Beautiful Springtime

美丽春天

Praise for *Raising Spring Kids*

Belinda Khong combines her expertise as a psychologist with her Asian cultural background to provide interesting teachings for our next generation of children so that they may be resilient, adjusted and happy in their lives.

Alister Henskens,
Senior Counsel, Member of Parliament
Member for Wahroonga, NSW, Australia

Raising Spring Kids by Dr. Belinda Siew Luan Khong focus on fostering spiritual and emotional growth in children through mindful parenting and supportive practices. The integration of poems, personal anecdotes, and practical exercises makes the book accessible and relatable to a broad audience, including parents, therapists, and educators. Her blend of Eastern wisdom and Western psychology offers a refreshing and balanced approach to child development. Highlighting children's innate qualities over deficits is an empowering and progressive narrative. The content is tailored to various contexts, ages, and cultural backgrounds, making it universally applicable. I enjoy the narrative depth. The vivid stories and examples effectively illustrate complex psychological and philosophical concepts in a tangible way.

Steven D. Smith, DPhil
Publisher, American Institute of Physics Publishing

Belinda Khong generously shares lessons from her therapy room, and beyond. She shares her teachings for children and adults alike. While it's a book about children, for children – it also offers the adult reader a unique experience. Whether as a therapist, parent, professional or just a "human being" (who finds their life intersects with children in some way or another, at any point) – adults are invited to take a reflective pause as they digest the wisdom distilled from spiritual traditions, and from the mouths of babes.

An interdisciplinary, intercultural, and intergenerational delight.

A humanistic and holistic approach to parenting and working with children – informed and inspired by mindfulness teachings and the wisdom traditions. Belinda offers a fresh, innovative approach for being fully present when relating with children.

The book is segmented into parts that are simultaneously simple to comprehend, and deep in their impact. Similarly, the contrast between Belinda's professional psychological explanations, and her grandson's youthful interpretations, creates an interplay between "serious" and "relaxed." Deeply profound and practical, at the same time. While Belinda authors the book, her grandsons were clearly involved in the collaborative and creative "endeavour" that is *Raising Spring Kids*. The interviews with Matthew and Nicholas add a whole other dimension to the richness of this text (see Nicholas' differentiation between Mindfull and Mindful in Chapter 7).

Each chapter of the book crafts a message of hope, with striking clarity. Underpinned by sound principles and yet also allowing the freedom for children to bring their beginner's mind (and spontaneous wisdom!) to each encounter. The cultivation of a growth mindset is a common thread throughout.

Belinda shares instructional and eclectic advice – as well as novel and sharp ideas – for mindful being and relating, as she marries eastern and western perspectives. A refreshing, sophisticated and unconventional read for anyone who is looking to elevate their own practice of mindfulness-in-action.

As a registered psychologist and mindfulness practitioner myself, I consider Belinda's book a touchstone for the embodiment and integration of teachings from Western psychology and Buddhist psychology. This book is a handy companion for any professionals who seek to imbed mindfulness into their therapeutic practice: whether that be mindfulness in client care, or self-care – or perhaps both. Mindfulness is positioned as a mindset, attitude, way of life, and (ongoing) choice.

Belinda blends the reflective wisdom from spiritual teachings, philosophy, modern psychology, case studies of childhood experiences, and decades of practical, tried-and-tested therapeutic maneuvers to shine a light on how we can nurture the Spring Kids in our lives. The book is filled with unexpected – playful and heartfelt – stories and moments, that transcend the traditional category of "parenting books". It is a valuable resource for adults working with children, adults parenting children – or equally, adults re-parenting themselves.

Emily Knowles
Organizational Psychologist,
Well-being Manager, Law Institute of Victoria,
National Convener, Buddhism and Psychology Interest Group,
Australian Psychological Society

We have enjoyed the writing process with Nai Nai, seeing her ideas develop through late nights and multiple iterations. Nai Nai's book is a natural balance between personal anecdotes and information. Filled with beautiful illustrations, this book is a heartfelt and educational guide for parents and kids alike.

Matthew & Nicholas D'Cruz

Foreword

It's an honor to write the foreword to this inspiring and remarkable book by noted psychologist, mindfulness teacher – and also my dear personal friend – Dr. Belinda Siew Luan Khong. Belinda's book offers readers an abundance of thoughtful advice, imaginative storytelling, heartfelt personal recollections, whimsical illustrations, poetry, and therapeutic vignettes. While intended as a parenting "advice" book, it's also a book children will enjoy and benefit from. Therapists, educators, and healthcare professionals will learn much from using the book.

More than anything, it's a deeply personal book. In almost every respect, its themes, illustrations, poetry, stories, and underlying philosophy draw richly from Belinda's Chinese heritage. Belinda shares the lessons about resilience she learned from her remarkable mother, who grew up under the hardship of the Japanese occupation of Malaya, and who recovered from a horrific accident that injured her and took her husband's life. She shares her personal experience of overcoming the childhood adversity imposed by a misdiagnosed stroke. She generously shares her daughter and grandchildren with us in her recollections of raising them as well as through their own delightful stories and drawings. She shares her wisdom as a therapist in inspiring tales of helping young patients develop and depend on their own inner resources. As a parent and therapist, Belinda does not "fix" children – she helps them surmount life difficulties by discovering their inner strengths.

As a psychologist, Belinda is best known for her pioneering work incorporating Buddhist principles into psychotherapy, and her Buddhist sensibility infuses every page of this book. This sensibility is apparent in her choice of parables and narratives (empty your teacup; the monk and the scorpion; Sakura and the cherry blossoms; the story of the Buddha's life and teachings), in her poetry (for example, "The Orchid"), and in Pip Tweed's illustrations, which at times creatively incorporate Zen-inspired inkbrush-style ensō. Belinda's Buddhist sensibility is most apparent, however, in the values the book epitomizes and embraces: the beginner's mind, mindfulness, generosity, and compassion.

The book is organized around the theme of raising children to be SPRING children (Spiritual, Positive, Resilient, Imaginative, Nimble, and Grateful) so they can grow up to become GREAT (Generous, Respectful, Empathetic, Appreciative, and Thoughtful). The ancient Chinese philosopher Mencius believed we are all born with the "seeds" of goodness within but that the seeds need watering and nurturing to grow. Belinda seems to be of the same mind, believing in children's innate capacity and desire to develop "Spring" and "Great" qualities when given the right kind of parenting.

Good parenting involves embodying Spring and Great qualities oneself – being a role model for one's children – and cultivating one's capacity for mindfulness – being able to listen and be fully present and responsive to their needs. This does not mean coddling or indulging them, and Belinda warns against overprotectiveness or dictating solutions to the problems they encounter. Instead, she encourages parents to help children unleash their natural creativity, discover their own solutions, and learn from their mistakes as they grow to become resourceful and resilient rather than vulnerable and fragile.

Most importantly, Belinda shows that good parenting does not have to be a grim undertaking; it can actually be fun. She demonstrates how it can be done through art, imaginative play, role-playing, storytelling, and helping children absorb the lessons nature has to offer. These are methods that enrich child and parent alike. The book is filled with useful examples of how to engage children in developing their character – examples parents can readily put into practice.

I used the word "character" in the previous sentence, and there is a way in which "character" has come to sound quaint and old-fashioned to modern ears. This is a tragedy, since, as the philosophers of antiquity knew, it is character that allows us to live happy lives individually and together as members of families and communities. This fundamental insight has gotten obscured as contemporary culture has focused increasingly on promoting the values of wealth, status, popularity, and fame that ultimately fail to promote genuine happiness and fulfillment. Belinda reminds us of what really matters – a good heart, a sense of our deep connection with others and nature, and the ability to rise to life's challenges – and provides parents with a guidebook that can help their children learn to manifest them in their daily lives.

Seth Zuihō Segall, PhD

Clinical psychologist and Zen Buddhist priest. Seth is a contributing editor for *Tricycle:* *The Buddhist Review,* **a member of the editorial board of** *The Humanistic Psychologist* **(APA), and author of** *Buddhism and Human Flourishing: A Modern Western Perspective* **(2020) and** *The House We Live In: Virtue, Wisdom, and Pluralism* **(2023)**

Acknowledgements

Many people have given generously of their time, support and encouragement in the creation and writing of *Raising Spring Kids*. I am deeply grateful to my daughter, Lynnette, and my grandsons, Matthew and Nicholas, for being on this journey with me, for sharing their stories and experiences, and most of all for being my wise critics and offering me timely feedback. This is a special year for Lynnette and Nicholas as they are both born in the Chinese zodiac year of the snake.

I thank my dear friend, Seth Zuihō Segall for his lovely Foreword which captures the essence of my book so well, and for his years of friendship and support in the area of work that we both enjoy.

I thank Steve D. Smith, a wonderful friend who understood my vision and encouraged me to write books which integrate my love of Eastern and Western wisdom and psychology, and for his guidance and mentoring of my writing.

I am grateful to my Member of Parliament, Alister Henskens for his generous and continuous support of my work. I thank my colleague, Emily Knowles, for supporting my vision in writing this book to help families, kids and therapists.

A deep bow of appreciation to my talented illustrator, Pip Tweed, who has magically transformed my ideas and writing into beautiful illustrations filled with humor, exquisite colors, laced with Chinese and Zen motifs. Pip is not only an amazing illustrator, but a dear colleague, who is always available at the end of the phone to listen and help me expound and expand on my themes and concepts.

I thank my book editor, Julie Ganner for her professional and wonderful editing, her mindful recommendations and for making the writing process more fun.

I thank my Chinese tutor, Kerry Wan, who patiently read my chapters and poems, and translated them into Chinese, and my friends Greg Li and Lydia Li who helped me with the Chinese translation of the poems.

A special thanks to my many clients, friends and colleagues who have shared their experiences with me, and allowed me to share their stories with others so that we can all learn and benefit from their amazing life journeys. I thank Acey, Harrison and Evie my young artists for their beautiful drawings.

In this book, I promoted the message that families are our greatest source of learning, healing and love. I am grateful to my parents, who have laid the foundation for what I do, and who I have become.

Finally, I am lucky to write this book in my Chinese, Zen-inspired home, which has inspired many of the Chinese and Zen themes in the book. My home has been a sanctuary and during the long hours of writing, and trying to unblock a "writer's block" offers a serene place to rest the mind and start anew each day with a beginner's mind.

INTRODUCTION

Now spring is here,
And I am a Spring kid again.
I like being a Spring kid
Why don't you give it a try?

– Extracts from "Ode to Spring Kids"
by Belinda Khong

Are you:

- concerned about the rising mental health crisis in kids?

- wanting to raise mindful kids?

- wanting to help your child reach their full potential?

- wanting to enhance how you engage with your child?

- looking to improve the way you communicate, work and collaborate with your child?

- looking for another approach to help your kids tap into their inner strengths to manage their problems in this fast-paced social media age of changing norms and values.

- looking for a way for the whole family to work together mindfully.

If you answered "Yes" to any of the statements above but are unsure how or where to start, your search ends here. My book, *Raising Spring Kids: A Psychologist's Guide to Nurturing Mindful Kids*, can show you how to raise and nurture children to be:

- Spiritual, Positive, Resilient, Imaginative, Nimble, and Grateful (SPRING)

- Generous, Respectful, Empathetic, Appreciative, and Thoughtful (GREAT).

This book is not just for parents. Therapists, educators, healthcare professionals, caregivers and anyone who raises and works with kids can benefit from using this strength-based guidebook which integrates mindfulness, the Buddha's teachings, and positive psychology. I use the terms "kid" interchangeably with "child," and "parents" with "every adult" who works with kids. I have also written this book using the US English style.

I have been working as a psychologist for more than 25 years, counseling hundreds of clients, young and old. I love my work. There is one major problem. I have deep concerns that we are failing our children. I am alarmed at the significant rise of mental health problems in kids – the over-diagnosis of mental health issues, including anxiety, attention deficit hyperactivity disorder (ADHD), depression, self-harm, eating disorder, gender dysphoria and so on – and the pathologizing of normal experiences such as sadness and stress as depression and anxiety disorders.

Prescription of psychiatric drugs to kids is also on the rise. I worry about the high level of antipsychotic drugs and Ritalin being prescribed to children in Australia. A 2021 study by Julie Klau and her colleagues at the University of Adelaide ("Prescribing of psychiatric drugs to Australian kids on the rise")[1] found that while few psychiatric drugs were approved for children and teenagers in Australia, between 2011 and 2018 the prescription of drugs for treating ADHD almost doubled, the prescription of antipsychotic drugs rose by 63 percent, and the prescription of antidepressants rose by 43 percent. These increases were the most significant in 10 to 14 age group.[2]

Significant amounts of government monies continue to fund the mental health sector in attempts to "fix" the problem. Despite these well-intentioned efforts from all quarters of society, the mental health crisis is rising, not falling. Children are diagnosed and offered solutions that often focus more on the symptoms rather than from understanding the young person holistically.

A recent article in *The Economist*, "How to stop over-medicalising mental health' (2023),[3] sounded the alarm that Britain is also over-medicalizing the population, including for mild forms of distress. The article argued that sometimes diagnosis and medication are not always the best answers, and that Britain has to be more thoughtful in dealing with mental health issues.

Young minds deserve more than pharmaceutical solutions. I believe that we can offer kids an approach that focuses on their strengths instead than on their deficits. My experience with my client, Nancy, and her daughter, Carol (aged 7) many years ago brought home these issues starkly.

I had been counseling Nancy, a young divorcee, for a number of years. Her daughter then began experiencing problems with concentrating in class, and was easily distracted. Carol was acting out in school, in defiance of the school authorities. Her doctor diagnosed her with ADHD and prescribed Ritalin. Nancy was reluctant to give Carol the drug, and took her to see a psychologist for an assessment. The psychologist also diagnosed Carol with ADHD and reported that she had a low IQ, based on the observation that she did not complete most of the items on the form and looked extremely bored during the entire assessment. Nancy was still concerned about putting Carol on Ritalin. She brought Carol to see me for a further consultation, and showed me the psychologist's report. I was shocked to read it. The psychologist even got Carol's gender and age wrong, identifying her as a 9-year-old boy.

I invited Carol to tell me more about the assessment and her schoolwork.

"I wanted the psychologist to just listen and talk to me," Carol explained. "But she kept asking me to fill up the form. It was so boring. So I stopped. It is the same at school and at home. The lessons in school are so easy. I want to learn about more interesting things. The homework is too easy. Mum is usually at work. So there is no one to talk to or play with at home."

"What do you do until Mum comes home?" I asked.

"I go outside and play with the kids," Carol replied. "I organize my friends to feed the birds and give them water to drink. I invent games with my friends to play with until Mum comes home. We collect old books and toys and ask our parents to donate them to children who needs them. I never get bored organizing these activities with my friends. I like helping people."

This is clearly a different picture of the child from the one presented in the report! Nancy and I took Carol to see the psychologist again. I shared with the psychologist what I learned about Carol from our discussion. The psychologist apologized for getting the reports of her different clients mixed up. She gave Carol another assessment and found that in fact she had a high IQ, approximately 140, which made her gifted. No wonder she found the assessment, schoolwork, and homework boring. She was not being creatively challenged or encouraged to talk about herself freely. The psychologist revised her report from a diagnosis of ADHD and low IQ to that of a creative, gifted child. Carol never took Ritalin, went on to complete university with high distinction. She is now a successful professional.

Imagine diagnosing well-founded boredom and a desire for creativity in a 7-year-old highly intelligent child as ADHD, warranting a prescription of Ritalin. While not all evaluations of kids are so far off the mark, I have encountered many, many wrong diagnoses of children over the years, causing me great disquiet. Carol's experience points to what can happen when therapists overlook the importance of practicing "a beginner's mind". This is an important attitude that the Buddha advocates: seeing everything afresh without making hasty assumptions and quick judgments about the other person. Parent–child communications are not immune to these kinds of cursory and often premature conclusions. I discuss the Buddha's teaching on the importance of cultivating a beginner's mind further in Chapter 7.

In *Raising Spring Kids*, I offer an innovative approach for working with young people, in contrast to the medical-based model of diagnosis, clinical assessment, and medication. I use this approach in my counseling of young clients and in teaching parents about mindful parenting, which is a major theme of this book.

What is mindful parenting? At the core of this style of parenting is bringing awareness to the present moment, a practice at the heart of the Buddhist concept of mindfulness. When you are a mindful parent, you keep an open, nonjudgmental mind about your children's experiences and try and understand their actions from their perspectives. While other parenting approaches tend to focus on teaching children about discipline, routine, and rights and wrongs (helpful as they are), mindful parenting encourages you to pause, and to respond – rather than react – to your child's behavior, with consideration and compassion both for your child and for yourself as a parent. A mindful parent helps kids build up skills to manage and regulate their emotions and feelings in more positive ways.

In this book, I provide many examples and exercises of mindful parenting that you can use with your kids. Being a mindful parent does not make you a perfect parent, or a parent who will never feel frustrated or annoyed with your child. However, parenting mindfully does make parenting less stressful, and you and your child less stressed.

In *Raising Spring Kids*, I integrate wisdom from Eastern and Western psychologies and philosophies alongside charismatic animal characters, captivating illustrations and inspiring poetry. These elements are designed to teach you how to use the themes in the acronyms SPRING and GREAT, so you can help your kids develop these positive qualities. With some assistance from you, older kids can also use the exercises in the book on their own to practice being a Spring and Great kid.

How do we know that the approach I recommend works? I have adopted this approach in working with children in, outside and beyond therapy for many years. In this book, I show how the positive values I address in Part 1 are reinforced in Part 2 and how I apply the values in working with my clients (Part 3). I also offer tips and practical exercises for you to use with your kids outside and beyond therapy (Part 4). Throughout my book, I utilize examples from both my clinical work and my own experiences of raising my daughter Lynnette and my grandsons Matthew and Nicholas. Most of the examples are transcribed from actual clinical sessions and my exchanges with the family. The accounts have been abbreviated in some instances, for clarity.

Regardless of your role in children's lives, I have structured the chapters so that you can use the book as a whole, and apply the key learnings from any part of it in your interactions with kids. I discuss the clinical vignettes at some length, giving a comprehensive account in order to maintain the integrity and unfolding of the counseling process. This is to provide you with a clearer picture of how I work with children, so you can use comparable techniques and skills when you communicate with your kids.

This groundbreaking book is the culmination of more than 25 years of my work as a psychologist and mindfulness and meditation teacher, and teaching mindful parenting to families. My adult clients have found the mindful parenting skills I taught them to be effective, and asked me to counsel their children. For example, I have worked with the parents of Georgia, Elizabeth, Wen, Shauna and Carol (whose cases are described in this book), and was gratified when they brought their children to consult with me. I have channeled the knowledge I have acquired from the work I do with parents and kids into the stories contained in this book.

The approach I take in this book blends my cultural heritage as a Malaysian-born, Australian-Chinese psychotherapist integrating important learnings from Eastern and Western psychologies and philosophies. The Buddha's teachings have parallels in the teachings of the great spiritual teachers – Jesus, Muhammad, Confucius, Lao Tzu, Mencius, and many others. You can seek out and also encourage your kids to explore comparable teachings, beliefs, and practices from different wisdom traditions. This book is suitable for adults and kids of varying ages, from any faith, culture, or background.

Personally, I have been involved with the Buddha's teachings, mindfulness, and meditation practices for most of my life. Growing up in Malaysia, where many of my family are followers of Buddhism, I would described myself as a "Sunday-school Buddhist": someone who accompanied my parents to temples and practiced acts of generosity to the monks and the Buddha on auspicious occasions. While it felt good, I did not understand much of the rationale for what I did. I merely carried out what my parents encouraged me to do. Then about 25 years ago, when I was researching Buddhist psychology and humanistic -existential psychology for my PhD thesis, I learned more about the Buddha's teachings. Since then, I have integrated and blended his teachings with psychology and psychotherapy extensively in my work and writings. In 2021, I was invited to be the co-guest editor of a double special issue on mindfulness for the American Psychological Association.[4]

I incorporate the Buddha's teachings in this book to show how they can help you and your kids to manage contemporary issues, and to open children's hearts to the practice of wisdom, compassion, gratitude and kindness. My approach is informed by the work and writings of eminent Buddhist monks and scholars such as Venerable Dr. K. S. Dhammaratana and Thich Nhat Hanh, and the work and writings of distinguished writers and researchers in the field of child development and mindful parenting including Jon Kabat-Zinn and Alison Gopnik.

Before becoming a psychologist, I practiced as a family lawyer. My experiences in this field have also influenced my philosophy in working with kids. I have witnessed enormous pain and psychological suffering when children are "caught" in family breakdown and custody issues. I have also witnessed children's strength and resilience in navigating problems that are seemingly beyond their tender years to handle.

Bearing witness to such suffering and hardship has motivated me to write a book that has as its guiding principles human strength, dignity, and courage. My counseling approach to use therapy as a dynamic, creative engagement – an art form – with my clients participating in the process as young researchers of their experiences, and as collaborators in the laboratories of their own learnings. While my book draws on clinical cases that are at times sad but always profound, these cases also attest to the resilience and wisdom found in children. I am continually touched and inspired by the kindness, empathy, and compassion of the young people I work with.

Raising Spring Kids showcases a cutting-edge, creative approach to nurturing kids. This approach is best captured by the dual meaning of "spring," a term I use as an analogy for working with young people:

- springtime – a season of change, renewal, and growth
- a spring mechanism with significant absorbent qualities, so that when families and kids are under stress – whether financial, emotional, or psychological – they can learn to adapt and bounce back.

In my line of work, I interact frequently with kids and have a strong desire to make a positive impact on their lives. I am continually reflecting on the question: "How I can give parents such as yourself a way to help your kid without making the child feel inadequate, isolated, or anxious?" This aspiration has motivated me to write books specifically designed to help children cultivate the deepening levels of psychosocial skills that are so essential to their overall development and well-being. My vision culminated in the publication of my series of Lunar New Year animal books for kids, a trilogy comprising *Am I a Tiger?* (2022), *Water Rabbit's Mindful Adventures* (2023), and *Dragon and Friends Mindful Adventures* (2023) which promote mindfulness, compassion, empathy, gratitude, and kindness.

Since the publication of the trilogy, I have been inundated with requests for advice. I am regularly asked: "How can we help our kids to reach their full potential?" and "Can you give us some guidelines?" So, in response to the growing demand for more books to help kids to flourish and thrive, I penned *Raising Spring Kids*. This book is an essential companion to my Lunar New Year animal trilogy. The animal friends who feature in the trilogy – water tiger cub, water rabbit, and wood dragon – act as "therapists," and join the Buddha to offer "a little help" to kids.

The Lunar New Year animal book series celebrates the birth of each animal according to the Chinese zodiac calendar: water tiger in 2022, water rabbit in 2023, and wood dragon in 2024. January 29, 2025 marks the birth of wood snake. I greet his birth in Chapter 17, where you can read about him and his relationship with his animal friends. You can also find out more about the wood snake, the Chinese Lunar New Year, the Chinese zodiac calendar and the zodiac animals in the "Explanatory notes from a Chinese perspective" at the end of this book.

Raising Spring Kids is structured in an accessible, easy-to-follow format laced with narratives and anecdotes that will help you learn how and where to start. In each chapter, I provide practical examples and recommendations for you to navigate the parent–child relationship, using simple exercises and actionable steps. Each chapter is also augmented by clearly expressed psychological concepts and explanations, key learnings, and practice guides.

How can you help your kids with their problems in a nondirective way? I have provided extensive clinical vignettes as examples to help you understand how to communicate with your kids mindfully. For example, in Chapter 17, when wood snake was born he experienced an identity crisis, wondering what kind of animal he was. The three animal friends brought wood snake to see me for "peer group counseling". Together, the animal friends – water tiger, water rabbit, wood dragon – and I helped baby snake discover himself.

This fictional counseling of an animal with an identity crisis shows how you can encourage your child to open up and talk about powerful emotions and feelings freely and safely, using the key learnings provided in Chapter 17.

For example:

- Be sensitive to kids' concerns about self-identity, self-understanding, peer acceptance and support.
- Explore with kids what they have learned about how the animals resolve their problems, and how they can use the insights to help themselves.
- Help your child to focus on what is good and positive about themself.

Animal friends peer group in counseling with Belinda.

Throughout this book, I have provided a wealth of stories, illustrations, and practice guide which you can use with young people on a range of issues.

Raising Spring Kids is an invitation and a love story. I invite you to embark on a journey that celebrates your parent–child relationship as one of the most special and endearing human relationships. I believe that every child is spiritual, beautiful, and authentic, and has a great capacity for kindness, empathy and compassion. I believe that every child possesses the inborn qualities of a Spring and Great kid. So each chapter honors the story of love and care between parents and kids; of mindful attending between therapist and client; of the love I received and the gratitude I owe to my daughter Lynnette and my grandsons Matthew and Nicholas, who embarked on this journey and worked tirelessly with me on the book; and of the love and devotion that every generation inherited from the previous generation and will pass down to the generation after.

This book is a road map for you to embrace kids fully as fellow travelers and to help them flourish as positive, confident, and contributing members of society.

Making the most of this book

How can this book help you raise mindful kids?

In my view, there is no blueprint or a "laundry list" for mindful parenting. However, my book gives you a framework for working with kids. The illustrated overview of Parts 1–4 gives you an outline of what each part of my book covers and the key learnings for you provided at the end of each chapter.

The chapters are enriched with stories of the work I do with my young clients, my daughter, my grandsons, and my encounters with individuals from all walks of life. Some of the anecdotes are deeply personal in nature, especially those of my mother and my own experiences. I had wondered whether these stories might be too personal. However, my grandson Nicholas assured me that people in his age group would benefit from reading about them.

"These stories are touching tales of hardship," Nicholas explained. "They are a worthwhile addition to your book, relevant and helpful, worthy of the reader's time. Yours and my great-grandmother's experiences can be learned from."

So to make the most of the stories in the book, take a leaf from Nicholas's advice, "learn from them," and enjoy the insights and inspiration you and your child will gain from the accounts.

Each chapter is accompanied by illustrations, wonderfully drawn with warmth, wit, and humor, bringing the stories to life and encouraging all to engage with the ideas pictorially. I invite you and your kids to actively participate in the book, using the illustrations as affirmations, flashcards, or prompts in ongoing discussions, and to gauge your child's understanding of the narratives. Sample practice exercises in Chapter 19 are provided for you and your family to enjoy learning to use this book together.

There is a significant Asian influence on the style and medium of the illustrations, which draw upon Chinese, Japanese, and Zen *ensō* (a circular form of drawing popularized in Zen art) elements and motifs. As with all my books, the color red is a constant and striking feature in the illustrations. You can find more information about the illustrations in the notes about the illustrations.

I have designed the book so that you can read it from the beginning to the end, in separate parts, or as individual chapters. However, I recommend that you first read the book as a whole, especially Part 4, and revisit each chapter depending on your current focus and interest. There is no right or wrong way to use this book. You are free to decide on the most effective way of doing so. References are available in the Notes if you wish to follow up with further reading.

Overview of the book

Raising Spring Kids is a highly readable and informative book to help you to engage with kids across a range of contexts. I hope it encourages you to pause and reflect on the human dignity and indominable spirit that unfold in the stories I share, especially those of the young clients I work with.

In Part 1, "Raising Spring Kids," I discuss the characteristics of each attribute in the acronym SPRING. In each chapter, I show how kids can be encouraged to cultivate these qualities. You can use, or adapt for use with your family, the humorous anecdotes and practical exercises.

Part 2, "Buddha and Animal Friends Talk to Kids," features entertaining vignettes adapted from the Buddha's life and teachings, Zen stories, and koans that I had shared with my grandsons Matthew and Nicholas from a young age. These stories and koans are frequently used to focus the mind on the central question asked for which there is often no simple answer; for example, "What is the sound of one hand clapping?"

The chapters in Part 2 include "Cultivating a beginner's mind: With mindfulness and meditation," "Right view and right action," "The monk and the scorpion," and "In Dreamland: Honesty is the best policy." In the vignettes, the Buddha and animal friends bring these stories and teachings to life with fun dialogue and relatable interactions. Matthew and Nicholas creatively made up their own stories based on the vignettes and discuss how the morals and the themes can be applied to contemporary issues faced by their peers. I encourage you to try out the stories and practices with your own kids as a way of helping them learn about deeper and more profound teachings that are usually not shared with the younger generation.

In Part 3, "Tales from therapy: Empowering kids," I discuss and illustrate through real clinical vignettes the somewhat unconventional approach I adopt in working with young people. This therapeutic method, which I describe as a person- and heart-centered approach, is not often employed by clinicians working with kids. This style of counseling focuses without judgment on what my clients share with me, and offers them practical, thought-provoking choices with clear boundaries.

The counseling accounts in Part 3 include "Kids are smarter than adults: How kids manage family conflicts," "Empowering kids through role-modeling: The teacup of gratitude," "Working with challenging kids: Playing ignorant," "The black sheep of the family: A label or a strategy?" and "'Am I a snake'? Exploring self-identity: Learnings from animal friends." While the people I worked with have generously consented to share their stories, I have changed their identities and personal information in order to protect their privacy. Despite the years that have passed, as I write about their stories, I am still deeply moved reliving the memories of my clients' quiet strength, empathy, and compassion, and the powerful insights they bring to the therapy sessions. The following are two heartwarming examples.

The parents of 8-year-old Wen (Chapter 11) were going through an acrimonious divorce, and Wen's father Sheng was undergoing treatment for advanced cancer. Wen was experiencing significant problems at school, but did not share with his teachers his emotional distress at home.

"My papa is sick," Wen explained. "Can you help him? I try to help him, but I am only 8 years old. I get very upset. I ask to go to bed. I can't finish my homework. My teachers get upset with me … But I can't tell them the real reason. It is okay if they get angry with me, instead of getting angry with Papa and Mama."

Looking tearful, Sheng spoke quietly. "Wen, thank you for showing us how to be kind and generous to each other. I will explain to your teachers why you didn't finish your homework, and why you were so sad at school. Today, I learned about how wonderful and beautiful my son is."

Wen turned to me. "Thank you for helping me and Papa today," he said. "I will finish my homework, and not hide things from Papa and Mama anymore. I feel better now."

Seven-year-old Georgia (Chapter 12) was an angry and highly anxious girl. Her reactions were responses to her parents' outbursts, her sense of helplessness, and her desire to make things better for the family. I helped Georgia design a list of "magic words" as circuit breakers to help her moderate her emotions.

At the conclusion of our counseling sessions, Georgia said: "You are trying to help me to understand why I get angry with Mummy and Daddy so much. It is when they get stressed or yell at me, or when I'm afraid or lonely. You taught me to help them to stop so that I won't feel so angry. I like that. I can learn not to be angry or stressed."

While the stories in Part 3 are situated in a counseling context, the insights, psychological explanations, and practice guides are equally applicable in nonclinical settings. I encourage you to adapt the techniques in your engagement with your kids.

Part 4, "Guide for Nurturing Mindful Kids," clears the clouds for you to enjoy the breathtaking rainbow and horizon at the end of the pathway to raising Spring and Great kids. Part 4 features easy-to-follow stories, advice, recommendations, and practice guides. Chapter 18 offers useful tips for practicing mindful communication, asking open-ended questions, resist fixing kids, and being a positive role model. Chapter 19 showcases sample practice exercises by kids and parents, and their explanations for their drawings, helping you learn how to use similar exercises with your families. Chapter 20 concludes the guidelines by offering anecdotes, advice and recommendations on how to raise Spring kids to become Great kids.

The illustrations in Part 4 afford you a way to use the tips and recommendations with your kids in imaginative, creative, and entertaining ways. I encourage you to read Part 4 regularly and to adapt the material to suit the age of your child.

There are four special features in this book. The first feature is the overarching message of the book: paying tribute to the wholesomeness of kids and animals, and blending their natural integrity with the wisdom and wise sayings from the great spiritual teachers.

The second feature is the constant presence of my grandsons Matthew and Nicholas walking alongside me as co-journeyers. They have helped me enormously with my animal trilogy books and are now important contributors to my current book. From a young age, Matthew and Nicholas have enjoyed learning to meditate with me and listening to the stories I tell them about the Buddha's teachings. They love curating stories with great wit and humor, applying the Buddha's teachings to the experiences of their peers and demonstrating how young minds understand complex concepts. This book is punctuated with anecdotes of our shared activities and experiences.

For example, Matthew and Nicholas, who have dual American-Australian citizenships, wanted to understand the difference between nationality and citizenship. I explained that Matthew, being born in America, could be the president and Nicholas, being born in

Australia, could be the prime minister. I was uncertain whether they understood the difference. However, Matthew and Nicholas demonstrated their considerable understanding in the role-play they created.

Matthew put out his hand. "Hello, I'm President Matthew. Nice to meet you."

"Hello, President Matthew. I'm Prime Minister Nicholas," Nicholas replied. "Welcome to Australia. Would you like a barbie?"

"I am a president. I do not play with Barbie dolls." Matthew pretended to look offended.

"'Barbie' is what we call barbecue in Australia. That is how we cook our meat," Nicholas explained.

"I am President Matthew."
"I am Prime Minister Nicholas. Have a Barbie!"

Matthew and Nicholas showed in their role-play that children are never too young to appreciate humor and the finer points of language, or to understand seemingly difficult concepts. You can use similar exercises to work with your child in exploring sophisticated ideas.

The third feature is the poems – the poetry of the renowned 13th-century Sufi poet Rumi, and the ones I composed to capture the emotions, heart, and soul of the stories. I have sprinkled my poems throughout the book. Read these poems quietly or aloud with your kids. Allow the images, sound, and rhythm of the verses to make the texts more engaging and to light up your child's imagination as you enjoy the book together.

The fourth and final special feature is the integration of rich Chinese cultural elements in the book. My poems are translated into Chinese to capture their universal appeal. The dedications to my mother and to Spring kids are beautifully drawn with Chinese details and motifs. I have curated the names of the main protagonists and animal friends from Chinese terms, with the exception of Sakura, a Japanese name. Many of the names I chose have personal and sentimental significance to me and my family. The translation and meaning of the poems and Chinese names are explained in the sections, "Spring kids in poetry" and "Explanatory notes from a Chinese perspective."

Finally, I offer this book as a gift to you. I hope that you enjoy reading it and that the insights kindle wonderful sharing, reflection, and contemplation.

Working with kids has been one of the most challenging, satisfying, and rewarding aspects of being a psychologist. Children have a natural curiosity, a wonderful "beginner's mind" about everything: their lives, families, friends, schools, and experiences; their fears, challenges, strengths, and joys. They also possess an amazing ability to find creative ways of managing their own problems, offer insightful explanations for their responses to and understanding of the world, and apply this understanding to daily experiences. The ability of children to be the authors and editors of their personal growth and flourishing is often untapped or written about in books about working with young people. I am constantly in awe of how much children can contribute toward their own learnings, and to the learnings of adults, when adults learn to appreciate the beauty and strength in each child.

Nothing in this book will ensure that your child will stop watching television when you ask them, or that the kids will not get under your skin, or that you will suddenly acquire the competence, energy, and patience to become a mindful parent. However, I hope that this book will help you appreciate and understand your child from a fresh, newfound perspective, so that the parenting journey becomes as the English romantic poet John Keats would have described it, "A thing of beauty is a joy forever," even when your kids push your buttons! My hope is that this book will nourish your relationship with your children, and that you enjoy walking together to the park in spring, summer, autumn (fall), and winter, instead of walking with them into my therapy room.

THE SPRING TREE

Part 1

Raising Spring Kids

A spring tree symbolizes the growth of a child. The diagram of the spring tree modeled on the birch growing in my garden gives a pictorial representation of the qualities that contribute to raising a Spring kid. The practice of mindfulness, like the soil the tree grows in, enriches it with essential nutrients. Being grateful – represented by the roots – is replenished by kindness, thankfulness, and appreciation, qualities which are in turn strengthened by continually practicing gratitude. Gratitude gives rise to the sprouting of the branches: being spiritual, positive, resilient, imaginative, and nimble. The leaves illustrate the flourishing of wisdom, insight, empathy, and compassion. The nutrients, roots, branches, and leaves are interdependent, each component nourishing the others, and being nourished in turn by the other components – a good example of interconnectedness, the idea of everything being part of the whole.

Part 1 offers a guide for how we can nurture kids to cultivate the qualities of being **S**piritual, **P**ositive, **R**esilient, **I**maginative, **N**imble, and **G**rateful: the essence of a Spring kid captured in the acronym SPRING. In Chapters 1–6, I explore each attribute illustrated in the spring tree diagram, recommend simple exercises and practices, and offer psychological explanations, key learnings, and a practice guide.

The SPRING acronym.

The chapters are augmented by the experiences of the personalities – real and fictional – who inspire the stories and are featured in the second row of the picture gallery (opposite page). By the end of Part 1, you will learn how to:

- use the practice exercises with your child.
- develop the skills to mindfully and effectively raise a Spring kid.
- use the techniques, psychological explanations, and key learnings to help your child build the foundation to become a Spring kid.
- reinforce your kid's positive values and behavior.
- act as a role model for your child, showing them how to embody and practice the qualities of a Spring kid.

The picture gallery.

Chapter 1

SPIRITUAL

**"No matter how small your action of kindness,
it will never be wasted."**

– Venerable Dr. K. S. Dhammaratana

What does it mean to be spiritual? What is a spiritual kid? How can you support your kids to be spiritual?

We speak often of the intelligent child. I believe that it is equally important to speak of the spiritual child. In his famous poem, "Two Kinds of Intelligence,"[5] the renowned 13th-century Sufi poet Rumi wrote about the different classifications of intelligence.[6]

According to Rumi, the first type of intelligence is usually acquired from books, schools, and external sources. While acquired intelligence is important, it is limited in its breath and depth as it is usually dependent on knowledge from others. The second kind of intelligence, Rumi explained, is one that comes from within yourself, like a fresh sparkling fountain flowing from the inside to the outside, constantly transforming and responding to external changes. Intelligence of this nature promotes spiritual growth, which is important to cultivate in children.

Being spiritual is a deeply personal and intrinsic quality. In my view, all children are born spiritual. This inborn capacity is an attitude that can be further strengthened through mindful nurturing. In this chapter, I discuss how you can nourish the qualities of a spiritual child from a psychologist's and parent's perspective, and how you can foster the kind of spiritual intelligence Rumi wrote about through simple exercises and practices.

In working with kids and my grandsons, it is evident that children are intuitively gifted with many wonderful attributes, including:

- a love of and attentiveness to nature, renewal, hope, and growth
- a respect and care for living things, big and small
- a sense of wonder, curiosity, empathy, and compassion
- an appreciation of the interconnectedness of things.

Our role as adults is to allow these qualities to manifest naturally, as they are important for kids' social development and relationships as they grow up and in their later years. I will elaborate further on this aspect in the psychological explanation and key learning sections of this book.

I recommend the following practices and exercises for you to try with your kids. These practices do not have to be complicated; you can use everyday happenings and activities.

A love of and attentiveness to nature, to renewal, hope, and growth

Adults, especially parents, tend to direct and at times intervene, often in the service of making things better, even when sometimes things are best left alone. We are all guilty of this tendency at times. This is the first kind of intelligence Rumi wrote about, and is acquired from external sources and people.

I encourage you to allow your children to enjoy spontaneously the wonders of renewal, hope, and growth – the themes of this book. Support your kids to embrace a simple love of and attentiveness to nature by encouraging them to experience what is happening in the here and now, a mindful awareness of things as they unfold.

I am an avid gardener and love growing orchids. During the flowering season, I encourage my grandsons Matthew and Nicholas to watch with me a yellow orchid blooming in the garden in spring. The essence of this exercise is captured in the poem I composed to celebrate the wondrous unfolding of nature.

The Orchid

Come and sit with me for a while,

As first my lips are closed and sealed,

Then my petals unfold one by one,

As I smile gently to greet the sun and rain.

First I show a dash of white,

Then some delicate brown freckles,

Finally my glorious show of yellow.

Please enjoy me lovingly,

As I enjoy you lovingly in return.

Please enjoy me, the orchid. As I smile gently to greet the sun and the rain.

When I share this exercise with my grandsons and with kids, I love seeing the look of awe and reverence on their faces as they experience transformation in nature. Renewal in nature gives kids hope of renewal in themselves. Kids often say to me, with the look of a child spellbound: "Look, the petals are uncurling slowly. The orchid is smiling at me. I don't have to do anything. The orchid is blooming all by itself."

You can use similar mindful exercises with your kids. For example, enjoy watching together how plants germinate from seedlings, or how a rainbow is formed from raindrops. These simple but deeply profound exercises help children learn to be spiritual and to experience nature unfold by letting things be.

A respect and care for living things, great and small

Growing up as a child in Malaysia, I was fortunate to learn to care for living things from my mother. My mother reared hens in a free-range environment. I would say that she was a naturalist when it comes to animal husbandry. Each morning, I would accompany her to the enclosure to feed the animals, clean their water troughs, and collect the eggs. My mother encouraged me to talk to the animals while I cleaned their shelters and fed them. She also taught me to lift each hen gently from its straw bed and check on the laid eggs. I was allowed to collect only the number of eggs we needed for breakfast, and told to leave the rest for "the mother hen to have baby chicks." My mother reminded me to thank the hens for the eggs. If any of the hens injured themselves, my mother would creatively fashion a splint from a small piece of wood and tie the cast gently on the injured hen until its broken leg was healed.

"Thank you for your eggs."

From a young age, my mother inspired me to respect living things, to care for them with love, and to be grateful for their gifts. I did not know then that I was being spiritual. However, I felt good for doing good. By fostering this spirit of respect and reverence, I believe my mother nurtured my sense of spirituality from a young age. Help your child embody and practice these simple acts of spirituality by role-modeling a similar attitude yourself.

A sense of wonder, curiosity, empathy, and compassion

As children grow up, they display a sense of wonder and curiosity about their world. The things and ideas you might take for granted, your child would wonder about. In Chapter 7, I describe this state of mind as a "beginner's mind": seeing things in a fresh and novel way. This sense of wonder and curiosity was demonstrated by my grandson Nicholas, who at 3 years old asked his meditation teacher: "Does the rainbow remember that it was a raindrop?" Nicholas said that he knew that the rainbow was a raindrop, but he wanted to know whether the rainbow knew. When you encourage kids to reflect on things from another's perspective, you are strengthening their capacity for empathy and compassion.

Let me illustrate.

When my grandson Matthew was 3½ years old, he and his mother Lynne encountered a wasp's nest near the house. The mother wasp rushed out to sting them. Matthew was scared, but also curious as to why the wasp wanted to attack him and his mother even though they were not near the nest.

"The mother is worried that we might hurt the baby wasps," Lynne explained. "She is only protecting her babies."

A few days later, I overheard Matthew telling a friend, "Don't hurt the wasps. The mother wasp

The mother wasp is worried. She is trying to protect her babies.

is worried. She is trying to protect her babies." Matthew appeared to be able to empathize with the mother wasp following the positive role-modeling he had experienced from his own mother.

Empathy and compassion are key elements of being spiritual. Sympathy and empathy are related but qualitatively different. Sympathy points to the ability to accept and acknowledge another person's feelings, but without necessarily sharing the same feelings. Empathy is the ability to understand and embrace the feelings of another person, to put oneself in the shoes of the other. Ideally, empathy leads to compassion.

Matthew's experience showed that when he was able to empathize with the fears of the mother wasp, he felt compassion in wishing to reduce its suffering by sharing his concerns with his friend. Kids are never too young to embody empathy and compassion if we are able to transform their beginner's mind in understanding profound learnings. Seek out simple happenings in nature for opportunities for you to role-model to kids how to be empathetic and kind. For example, you could invite your kids to put out a bowl of water in the garden for the animals and birds, or teach them to be mindful about not stepping on small insects when they walk.

An appreciation for the interconnectedness of things

An essential part of being spiritual is to appreciate that we are part of a whole: we are all interconnected and each of us contributes in unique ways to the mystery of life. Accepting that we are but part of a whole brings a sense of humility and grace. Help your child to appreciate their sense of spirituality and deep connection by experiencing this truth simply. Again, nature is a wonderful teacher.

The renowned Buddhist monk and mindfulness teacher Thich Nhat Hanh wrote a poignant article[7,8] on interconnectedness in his conversation with a leaf. Nhat Hanh recounted how he asked a fallen leaf how it felt in autumn (fall), away from the tree. He said that the leaf expressed no fear as it had become part of the tree, having sustained it during the growing months. It would now go back into the soil to nourish the tree for new growth in the next spring.

Nhat Hanh's narrative is a wonderful expression of interconnectedness, which is a major theme in my book. His commentary brought back wonderful memories of my own encounter with how things are interdependent. I have a rose garden, where I would often pick roses for my flower arrangements. I usually looked for fresh blooms. One day, I observed my own mind searching for only newly opened roses and ignoring the dead flowers on the ground. In a moment of mindful awareness, I realized that I had lost sight of the fact that the dead flowers came from the rose bush and would go back to nourish it. I had unwittingly judged one component of the whole to be more important or more beautiful than another component. In that moment, I realized that I was not being spiritual and had lost a crucial understanding of the intimate connection with growth, life, death, and renewal.

The leaf goes back to the soil to nourish the tree for new growth.

The rose encounter has stayed with me to this day, and I have never made the same mistake again. I made a practice, as I walk in nature, to observe my judging and discriminatory mind. It is helpful for us to understand that being spiritual involves remaining present with what is unfolding without judging some things as "good" or "bad," "worthy" or "unworthy."

Interconnectedness can be a difficult experience to teach kids, but it is an essential learning in their being spiritual. Nhat Hanh's encounter with the autumn leaf is an exercise that you can easily reproduce with your children. In autumn, take them for a walk to observe a deciduous tree. Ask them, for example, "What happens to the leaf when it falls to the ground?" "How do you think the leaf and the tree feel?" What happens to the leaf and the tree in spring?" In Chapter 6 (on being grateful) I have provided further examples for you to help your kids appreciate the subtle and often humbling experience of feeling part of the whole. Try these exercises with your family. You will be amazed at the insights you and your children will gain.

Psychological Explanations and Key Learnings

Nurturing kids to get in touch with their sense of being spiritual, and helping them to embody this quality, is important for their psychological and emotional development both as kids and later as adults. Being spiritual is both a practice and an attitude.

Kids are spiritual. We do not have to instruct them in this important expression. We just have to allow them to get in touch with the experience (as opposed to the theoretical knowledge) of love, care, respect, reverence, empathy, compassion, and interdependence. In this chapter, I have shown how you can employ ordinary and uncomplicated exercises to help your kids cultivate these attributes. However, remember to keep your role to a minimum. While you can initiate and facilitate the exercises, it is important that you encourage your kids to discover the key learnings and insights themselves.

As children grow up, being spiritual will strengthen their social relationships. I often hear concerns about the lack of respect and consideration being shown by younger people to the older generation. At the same time, elders are advised to show respect to kids. Rightly so. However, respect needs to be a two-way street.

Encourage your kids from a young age to practice respect for living things, great and small, as my mother taught me to respect the mother hen. Encourage them to appreciate nature, as Nhat Hanh taught us to appreciate the nourishing connection between the leaf and the tree.

Similarly, if we bring up children from a young age to appreciate that they were brought into the world by their parents, and that they will in turn look after them, mutual respect will develop naturally. I believe that if we have dignity, we will treat others with dignity, as we will be less focused on our own importance. If we have self-respect, we will respect others, as we are humble enough to know what we do not know. When we teach our kids to care for the innocent and the vulnerable with dignity and respect, we are also teaching them to look after the previous generations who looked after them when they were young. Practicing this attitude is good for kids and for humanity. It is that simple!

Practice Guide

- Keep the exercises and practices simple and interesting.

- Work with everyday activities that are easy to organize.

- Encourage children to get in touch with nature freely, without prior instructions or expectations.

- Allow your kids to take the lead and you join in as a co-explorer.

- Encourage children to discover the more profound insights for themselves.

- Encourage kids to take their respect and reverence for and interconnectedness with the natural world, and extend this to humanity.

Chapter 2

POSITIVE

Nourishing a positive attitude
in a challenging world.

"Life can be full of challenges. If you face them with a sense
of humor, you will find joy even in the toughest moments."

– Master Sito

Mastering happiness and success: The watermelon lesson[9]

Like carrying a watermelon, life can be full of challenges. Having a sense of humor helps.

Long ago, in a small village, lived a wise monk called Master Sito. The monk was well known for his simple wisdom and sense of humor. One day, a young boy named Song asked Master Sito to teach him the secret of happiness and success. Master Sito agreed, but he asked Song to first complete the simple task of buying a big, juicy watermelon, carrying it on his head and walking through the village without dropping the fruit.

Song was puzzled but did as he was told. The villagers were amused by the sight of the little boy in deep concentration, walking with a watermelon balanced on his head. The villagers laughed, clapped and cheered him on. Finally, after a difficult journey, Song reached Master Sito with the watermelon intact. Upon seeing Song, Master Sito burst into laughter.

"The secret to happiness and success is simple," he told Song. "Like carrying that watermelon, life can be full of challenges and unexpected twists. But if you face them with a light heart and a sense of humor, you will find joy even in the toughest moments."

Song laughed too as he realized the wisdom in Master Sito's advice. From then on, whenever Song felt sad or overwhelmed, he would remember the funny watermelon lesson and find the strength to keep going.

As the watermelon story shows, everyone experiences life's challenges from time to time. The moral of the story is to try and respond to these challenges with a positive attitude and with resilience, determination, and a sense of humor.

In Chapter 1, I wrote about supporting kids in strengthening their sense of spirituality.

Helping kids to cultivate a positive attitude is equally crucial. What are some of the qualities of being positive? How can you help your child to develop a positive attitude? In this chapter, I discuss the essential qualities associated with this attribute.

It is not possible or desirable to shelter your kids from negative or difficult experiences, as doing so will lessen their capacity to cope or to develop resilience. You could, however, help them acquire a sense of optimism and hopefulness. When kids embrace positivity as a habitual everyday mindset, they have a good foundation to navigate life's ups and downs.

Why is this important? A positive attitude gives your kids a sense of self-worth and self-esteem, and the capacity to manage their own emotions. I believe that children are born with a healthy optimism towards life and the ability to persevere and overcome obstacles. You only have to look at your child's determination in learning to talk, walk, and run to be inspired by their sense of confidence and a "can-do" attitude. This is why it is easiest to foster a positive mindset in your kids in their formative years, when they are open to new learning and experiences.

Helping your kids embrace and manage their emotions

Cultivating a positive attitude in your child does not mean eliminating negativity. Our emotions and feelings are not binary, an "either/or" state; they are situated on a continuum. Encourage your kids to embrace all aspects of themselves – the good, the bad, and the neutral. And when your child experiences ups and downs, let them know that it is okay not to feel okay all the time. Offer up healthy ways to help your child manage difficult situations with confidence and competence.

The exercises you initiate need to be tailored to your child's level of comprehension so they learn to develop personal coping skills. Take the example of when they fall down and tell you they are hurting. At times, you might try and pacify your child, saying, "It's okay, it doesn't hurt much." This kind of response could have the unintended consequence of giving your kid the impression that their feelings are not understood or are discounted. The child might end up placing more reliance on you telling them how they feel than on how they really feel. The same reasoning applies to when kids feel sad, angry, depressed, anxious, or frightened.

Children need to learn how to get in touch with and express their feelings and emotions. With younger kids, you can try this simple game. When your child indicates that they are hurting, use a favorite toy – for example, a teddy bear – and encourage them to ask Teddy how it is feeling. "Tell me where it hurts, Teddy?" or "Is Teddy scared?" Encourage your child to give Teddy a favorite blanket or a snack to make it feel better. You can then invite Teddy to ask your child similar questions and let them respond directly to Teddy.

"Tell me where it hurts, Teddy?"

You can encourage your child to check in again with how Teddy is feeling. In this to and fro exchange between kids and their favorite toy, you are giving them a fun medium to explore their feelings, learn to take charge by tending to another's problems, and gain self-confidence in doing so.

With older kids, you could help them get in touch with unexpressed feelings by labeling their feelings through drawings, illustrated flashcards, or made-up stories. You can also assist children to manage their emotions and feelings through mindfulness and meditation exercises, such as those I taught my grandsons (see Chapter 7). Help your child to manage negative emotions and thoughts through these simple exercises: releasing their emotions and thoughts into balloons or soap bubbles and letting the thoughts float to the sky, or replacing negative thoughts with happy memories.

In my clinical practice, I designed two interesting exercises to help my clients manage difficult or negative feelings. The first one, "the handbag exercise," involves the client naming the feeling, opening the handbag, briefcase or laptop, putting the feeling inside and locking the bag. The other, "the hot-water bottle exercise," involves clients using their handbag or a cushion as an imaginary hot-water bottle and placing the item on the part of their bodies where they are experiencing negative feelings. They can also send loving kindness to the feelings. I encouraged my clients to imagine the warmth soothing their feelings. These exercises work particularly well for clients who are experiencing anxiety, stress, and panic attacks.

You can adapt these exercises to use with kids. For example, you can substitute the handbag with a school bag, backpack, or a musical instrument case. The hot-water bottle can be replaced with a blanket, pillow, soft toy, or any object that gives an imagined sense of warmth. The crucial ingredient is to ensure that the exercises are easy to organize and to use. Like when Master Sito asked Song to balance a big watermelon on his head, it is important that you and your child enjoy the lightheartedness in the exercise and allow humor to break the cycle of negativity. When you help your kids to cultivate a positive attitude, you are encouraging them to accept where and how they are, and reinforcing their ability to cope with their emotions.

Building a sense of optimism and hopefulness in kids

To maintain a positive outlook, kids need to be optimistic and hopeful about the future, and to gain confidence that they can make a difference to outcomes. When kids encounter adverse experiences, negative self-talk, such as "I am a failure" or "I am worthless," often arises. Such self-talk impacts negatively on children's self-confidence and engenders feelings of learned helplessness.

Learned helplessness is a psychological state uncovered by the American psychologist Martin Seligman,[10] who developed positive psychology. Seligman conducted a series of experiments with dogs. He observed that when the dogs were repeatedly exposed to

adverse surroundings with no chance of escaping them, the dogs ultimately gave up trying to leave, even when the opportunity to do so became available. The dogs had learned to accept helplessness and psychological defeat. Learned helplessness – or, to put it in lay terms, "What is the use of trying?" – is a state of mind you can help your kids avoid if you support them to gain a sense of control over their feelings, actions, and behaviors.

The exercises you use to for build this sense of optimism and hopefulness can be similar to those I described earlier. But any simple exercise of mindfulness, meditation, creativity, or volunteering can also be helpful. Tailor the activity at a level your child is able to sustain. For example, in the case of meditation, if your child's maximum concentration span is about 10 to 15 minutes, let them practice for 8 to 10 minutes in order to build a sense of proficiency and give them confidence that they are able to finish the task.

Helping kids make a positive difference by giving and sharing

When kids know they can make a positive difference to their lives and the lives of others, they develop a healthy sense of agency that acts as a buffer against the feelings of helplessness I described earlier. It is never too early to help your children cultivate this kind of attitude. Simple acts of giving and sharing can start them on this journey of generosity.

One of the complaints I hear regularly from parents is that kids nowadays have too many presents and devices, often gifted at birthdays, Christmas, and other special occasions. You may have witnessed kids getting lots of books, Lego, Barbie dolls, computer games and so on. You would also have seen young children appearing to be more interested in playing with the inexpensive wrapping paper than the more expensive present inside. And you may have encountered kids calling out to embarrassed parents in toy shops and supermarkets: "I want, I want!"

So how do we change this kind of behavior? The solution is quite simple: encourage acts of giving and sharing instead of buying your kids more toys. "But how?" you might ask.

Let me share some simple practices you can adopt with your children. From a young age, I encouraged my grandsons Matthew and Nicholas to practice giving and sharing. For example, on their birthdays and special occasions, instead of buying them presents, I would purchase gift vouchers in their names from charitable organizations such as The Smith Family, the Kids with Cancer Foundation and World Vision. These organizations usually mailed out a thank-you card to Matthew and Nicholas. Later, my grandsons and I would log on to the charity's website and purchase books for children of a similar age using their vouchers. In this way, the boys learned to gift books to less advantaged children. I also opened a bank account where they could deposit the cash presents I gift them at Lunar New Year. I encourage them to set aside 10 percent of the cash to donate to a charity of their choice.

At home, you can also encourage your kids to share. I have shown in Chapter 13 how I helped my young client Georgia (aged 7 years) experience the joy of giving by sharing the stars she earned through good behavior with her family. This simple practice helped Georgia manage her emotional issues of anger and anxiety.

I also encourage Matthew and Nicholas to share with each other.[11]

On my meditation teacher's birthday, Matthew donated his entire savings of two $1 coins to my teacher as a hong pao (a Chinese term for a lucky money present). Nicholas was sad.

"I don't have a present to give to Bhante [a Pali term for teacher]," he explained. "I used my savings to buy my brother a birthday present last month."

"It's okay, Nicholas," Matthew replied, "you can share my present. I'll give Bhante a $1 coin on your behalf."

Bhante was touched and the boys were both happy.

"Nicholas, you can share my present. I will give
Bhante a $1 coin on your behalf."

You can introduce such uncomplicated acts of sharing with your children and afford them the opportunities to experience the joy of giving. Your kids will also learn to appreciate what they have, and to empathize with others less fortunate than themselves. My advice to you is to encourage restraint in your kids. Allow them to differentiate between what they need from what they want by motivating them to help others.

Psychological Explanations and Key Learnings

In today's challenging world, you might ask: "How do I help my child to embody a positive attitude? Can I give them hope for a better future?" The short answer is "Yes." I am concerned that apart from navigating the demands of growing up, our kids are constantly made to feel anxious about the problems of the world – problems that are fundamentally adult issues such as gender, sexuality, wars, conflicts, and climate emergencies. It is not surprising then when we hear kids lamenting: "What is the point of studying, playing sports, or helping? The world is going to end soon because of global warming, wars."

It saddens me very much when I encounter such despair and hopelessness in kids, and the loss of innocence. This is especially so when children are constantly exposed to information about, for example, how our country is racist, that our forefathers ruined the current generation, or how the world is being destroyed by changes to the climate.

How can you encourage your kids to remain positive when all they hear is how negative or bad everything is? I am not suggesting that we cocoon children in a Pollyanna world and keep them naive. What I am recommending is that you can support your kids to appreciate "The power of one" – that each of them can make a positive difference.

I recall that when I was writing an article[12] on responsibility and compassion, I had a conversation with Matthew, who was then 4 years old. He described his love for the family and his awareness of his personal limitations.

"I love everyone so much in my heart," he said. "But I'm only 4 years old. I have a small heart, and I love so MANY people. Sometimes I worry about the people that I love. It is in my heart."

As Matthew showed so poignantly, kids have a natural capacity to love and to care. Their worldview is one of goodness and unconditional love. This is the kind of world I encourage you to inspire your kids to dwell in. Share with them the story of Malala Yousafzai,[13] one of the recipients of the 2014 Nobel Peace Prize, who made a positive change by standing up to the Taliban and advocating for the education for girls.

We have to let kids be kids. Helping children feel positive about themselves and the world around them is the best legacy you can give them when they are young.

Practice Guide

- Keep the exercises and practices simple and entertaining.

- Use everyday activities that kids can relate to.

- Encourage your children to:
  - design their own exercises for managing their emotions and practicing acts of generosity
  - talk about how they feel about giving and sharing
  - use inspiring individuals as role models
  - explore how they can make a positive difference.

Chapter 3

RESILIENT

Building resilience for psychological
and emotional well-being.

**In loving memory of my mother, Yin Hong Har
– a special Spring kid and resilient role model.**

In my view, resilience is one of the most essential attributes we can help kids to cultivate. I addressed being spiritual and positive in Chapters 1 and 2. Fostering resilience is to give a child the third pillar in the triangle of psychological well-being – the third character strength of a Spring kid.

What does it mean to be resilient? How do we help kids to develop this important quality?

Resilience embodies both physical and emotional fortitude. In this chapter, I focus primarily on emotional resilience. This book and this chapter in particular is dedicated to my mother, who role-modeled resilience to me when I was growing up.

What is resilience?

For different people, resilience can mean different things depending on various factors including age, culture, beliefs, religion, upbringing, socioeconomic status, social considerations, and lived experiences. Generally, being resilient speaks to an ability to manage and overcome adversities and obstacles, and to bounce back from challenging situations with adaptability and agility. I believe that being resilient is both an innate capacity and a learned skill. It is associated with a healthy sense of self-confidence, self-belief, competence, and an inner strength.

You might find some of the synonyms for resilience helpful. Resilience encompasses flexibility, springiness, spring, and hardiness. Flexibility is the ability to adapt easily in response to changing situations. Springiness is being supple and capable of returning to the original form after being stretched or bent. Spring denotes both the season of growth following the inactivity of winter and a spring mechanism that has significant shock-absorbent qualities. Hardiness refers to the ability to cope with difficult or adverse situations. Hence, being resilient involves flexibility, adaptability, and resourcefulness.

The Resilient Brigade.

The following stories reflect the resilience of my young client, my mother, and myself. I hope you will share the anecdotes with your kids and inspire them to cultivate this invaluable life skill.

A resilient kid: Elizabeth's story

Elizabeth was a 13-year-old client I had been counseling for several months. (I share her story at length in Chapters 15 and 16.) She was experiencing significant psychological and emotional issues resulting from major problems at home and in school. When I first started working with Elizabeth, she was defensive and unyielding. Nevertheless, the fact that she did not fall apart prior to counseling suggested to me that she possessed an inner resilience. However, Elizabeth did not seem able to draw on this inner strength as she lacked confidence and the self-belief that she could make a difference to her situation. She saw the world in concrete, black and white terms: "You are either for me or against me." She often reacted by acting out – being "the black sheep" of the family or rebelling against school rules.

My counseling approach was to help her to use her coping skills in positive ways. I offered Elizabeth the "three options" strategy (see Chapter 16): giving her the choice of continuing to fail in school and being expelled again, rebelling against school rules, or taking on the challenge to follow school rules and improve her grades. Elizabeth rose to the challenge, changed her attitude, and thrived. Her mother Rosalind told me about the change.

"Elizabeth is doing really well at school," she said. "Her grades have all gone up, and she is excelling at all her subjects … She follows all the school rules. She is nicer to all the family members. She seems to be happier, calmer, less depressed, and less stressed."

"Your daughter is an intelligent, highly creative person," I replied. "All I did was trust her, appeal to her sense of integrity and fair play. And I helped her realize that being a strong, positive teenager is better than being the black sheep of the family."

By being encouraged to tap into her resilience and then strengthen this attribute, Elizabeth learned to be more flexible and to adapt, rather than react, to her circumstances. In building up her self-belief and confidence, she was able to bounce back to her positive self – the true character of a Spring kid.

In the same way, you can help your kids become more resilient by encouraging them to tap into their inner resources.

A resilient role model: My mother's story

My mother is my inspiration and role model when it comes to resilience. Writing about her experiences serves as a constant reminder of her courage and spirit.

My mother was born in 1926, the eldest of 13 children. Life was hard for her. During the Second World War, when Malaysia (Malaya as it was known then) came under Japanese occupation, life got harder. My mother had to leave school, having only completed her primary education, to help my grandparents look after her younger siblings.

As a child, I listened to her stories of having to venture out under the cover of night to scrounge for eggs, chickens, and even wild animals in the jungle; to dig out potatoes and other root vegetables; and to draw water from the nearby pond for the family's daily needs. My mother also told us of the time she was crowned Miss Kedah at a beauty contest organized by volunteers for the state of Kedah in Malaysia, to raise funds for the war effort.

My mother when she was crowned Miss Kedah, aged 17 years.

I enjoyed listening to her exciting stories. Until I was older, I didn't realize how many times she had escaped being killed. This was because I never heard her complain of the occasions she went hungry or had to hide in an old dry well for fear of being captured. As a young child, my mother's experiences felt like an interesting story, like watching a movie. But even then, I sensed that she was an amazing person. I just did not appreciate just how amazing!

After the war, my mother married my father; she was 18 years old and he was 20. They

My mother and I sharing stories about her life.

raised six children, of which I was the middle child, and enjoyed being grandparents to 14 grandchildren. Life was easier and more pleasant than during the war. But then, when my father was 70, a monumental tragedy struck our family.

My father was retired, and my parents would often visit a popular Malaysian mountain resort called Genting Highlands. On June 30, 1995, they took a taxi to the resort for a holiday. On their way, a massive landslide caused by heavy monsoon rain washed away the roads. We learned later that overdevelopment at the resort had contributed to the avalanche that led the hillside to collapse.

The following is an abridged version of the accident as reported in the local newspaper:

KUALA LUMPUR, June 30 – A devastating landslide killed 17 people, including a baby, and injured 23 near the Malaysian capital. ... [T]he slide buried 10 to 15 cars under tons of earth on a road. ... Other vehicles tumbled down a ravine. ... Some of the bodies were recovered from the mangled vehicles, some had been washed down the ravine. Rescuers with the help of spotlights were working through the night looking for survivors. ... [V]ictims remained trapped in vehicles that were swept down the ravine and also because of the severity of the injuries among the rescued victims. Most of those injured in the landslide were in a critical condition and unconscious ("Landslide kills 17 in Malaysia," July 1, 1995).[14]

The taxi driver who drove my parents was lucky to get out of the taxi before it was washed into a deep ravine. My parents were not so fortunate. My father was among the 17 people killed, and my mother was one of the 23 people seriously injured. My father had a heart attack instantly when the taxi tumbled over the hill.

As devastating as the loss of my father was, my mother's will to live was remarkable. We learned later that when the taxi fell into the ravine, my mother managed to kick herself out of the car boot, as the car doors were held shut by the murky water. She shouted out to the rescuers: "I am here! I am here!" The rescuers managed to save her, incredulous that a 68-year-old woman could push herself out of the boot. She even had the presence of mind to borrow a rescuer's mobile phone to call and let us know she had been rescued.

My mother spent one month in intensive care, as her lungs were filled with water and sediment. My family and I were concerned that she might experience post-traumatic stress disorder (PTSD) from the tragic loss of my father and the terrible accident itself. However, we had not counted on her incredible fortitude. She explained that although she was devastated, she was comforted that my father had died from the heart attack instantly, as it meant he suffered less when the taxi hit the water than he might otherwise have done had he been badly injured. She also advised us that she wanted to organize a Buddhist funeral service for my father, as he would have wanted. She attended the funeral in a wheelchair, temporarily released from hospital for the service.

In 2015, my mother passed away from cancer, 20 years after the tragic accident. Up to her death, she remained reflective and composed, saying: "When the earth is ready for me, I am ready to go. I have no fear of death. I accept that it is inevitable."

After my mother's passing, I wrote about her experience with cancer, and her attitude to life and death.[15] However, no written word can capture her resilience, her inner strength, and her ability to remain positive in the midst of terrible tragedies. Maybe the war years gave her the ability to bounce back, again and again. Maybe her love of nature and her spirituality – qualities she gifted me and which I wrote about in Chapter 1 – gave her strength and courage.

I will never know. But this I do know: my mother, regardless of her age, was the embodiment of a Spring kid. The war may have cut short her education, the landslide may have taken away her husband, and the cancer her final breath. However, none of the traumas she experienced took away her spirit to live and her capacity to cope without feeling sorry for herself or feeling like a victim. From my mother, I learned that it is not what life pitches to you. It is how you learn to catch the ball and to pitch back.

The intergenerational legacies my mother gifted me shine for me today as brightly as they did in the days when I sat by her side and listened to her stories of never giving up. I have recounted my mother's experiences to my daughter and my grandsons, and they are also inspired by her resilience. I encourage you to share your and your family's accounts of resilience with your kids. I am certain they will gain much from the sharing.

My experience with being resilient

As a child, when I was learning to walk, I kept falling down. My parents realized that something was not quite right. Over the years, I was diagnosed by various doctors as suffering from everything from a leg fracture, muscular dystrophy, and tuberculosis of the bone to polio and post-polio syndrome.

Many years later after I moved to Sydney, I learned from a prominent neurologist that all the earlier diagnoses had been wrong and that I had in fact suffered a childhood stroke. I also discovered that had the correct diagnosis been made, and had I received the appropriate treatment, the physical effects would have been much reduced. As it is, the childhood stroke left me with a general weakness and pain in the left side and back of my body which persists until today, and which I now manage with physiotherapy and hydrotherapy.

Back in Malaysia, I attended a Catholic school. Generally, while my disability was painful, it did not cause me much concern except when other people commented on my walking, asking me to straighten up and to walk "properly." I usually walked to school, a distance of 3 kilometers each way. As I grew older, I cycled to school with my siblings. They rode big bicycles while I rode a bicycle with training wheels, to help with my balance. Nevertheless, I was happy, being able to be with my older siblings and being treated like every other kid.

It was on the sports field that my disability caused me the most distress. When I was 8 years old, due to my inability to run fast, most of my classmates did not want me to join their team. They said I would slow them down, and that we might lose the race. While I appreciate that they did not mean to be unkind – they just wanted to win – the rejection by my peers hurt. This experience went on for some time until I dreaded attending sports days or physical education (PE) classes. Hoping to spare me further emotional distress, my PE teacher recommended that I either use the library or the art room during the classes.

This recommendation worked well. During PE classes, I alternated between reading books in the library and drawing in the art room – both of which activities I love and have stood me in good stead to this day.

However, the feelings of rejection never really went away. I remember one sports day, hearing the laughter and cheers while I sat in the library. I closed the door, hoping to shut out the noise, but I couldn't shut down my internal dialogue.

"I wish that I could join them. It is NOT fair."

"I wish I could join them. It is NOT fair."

As the tears ran down my cheeks, something opened up in my heart and mind. I stopped crying. I remembered saying quietly and firmly to myself, "I deserve better. I will not let their rejection get me down. I will overcome this and prevail." And I believed I could.

Young as I was then, I resolved to focus on my intellect rather than on my physical disability. I went on to become a school prefect, earned a law degree and a PhD in psychology, and practiced as a psychologist. I am currently writing books that I hope will help kids to reach their true potential.

In hindsight, I think that my newfound resolution came when I stopped feeling sorry for myself. I also realized that I was not going to let others' ignorance and insensitive behavior determine the course of my life. I learned to strengthen my inner resolve to rise above my present circumstances. I am not sure where this sense of resilience came from. Perhaps it is an innate ability I always possessed. Perhaps it is from the years of role-modeling I received from my mother. I am certain that her philosophy and positive attitude permeated my psyche and came to the fore when I needed to trust in myself. Certainly, it has reinforced my belief in positive role-modeling, and why I promote this theme so extensively in my writings.

I also recalled the Buddha's advice: "As a human being, physical suffering is at times inevitable. But emotional suffering is optional. It is how you respond to the suffering that is important."

Nowadays, we often hear and read about kids being bullied and harassed in school or on social media by other children, and the negative impact these experiences have on their mental health. Your child may have encountered similar behaviors too. I share my experiences to encourage you to help your kids see that they are defined not by the challenges they encounter, but rather by how they respond to them.

You can support your kids in coping with negative actions from their peers by helping them to:

- appreciate, as I have learned, that sometimes people may be acting more from ignorance rather than malice

- not see themselves as victims, and to use their inner strengths and resilience to transcend the situation

- not let others define who they are and what they choose to be.

My mother has given me many special gifts. We were both born in the Chinese zodiac Year of the Tiger, from which I probably inherited her indomitable spirit. Both our Chinese names, Luan-Feng (栾 峰), mean phoenix, a mythical bird from Chinese legends, which speaks to our love for nature and beautiful things. However, I believe that the best gift my mother bequeathed me was her inner strength and her sense of empathy and compassion. On reflection, the painful experiences I went through growing up turned out to be a blessing. Like my mother, these experiences have helped me empathize and care for the young and the vulnerable.

When I shared this chapter with my grandson Nicholas, he remarked: "Kids like us need to hear such stories. We think that our lives are difficult. However, it sounds like my great-grandmother and you had more difficult lives. We can learn from them." Similarly, you can role-model for your kids how you have coped with and transcended negative experiences, and what you have gained from adversities. In this way, you can help your child transform hardships into learning opportunities.

Helping kids to cope and be resilient

How can you help your kids strengthen their sense of resilience? What role can you play in this important development? Here are some of my recommendations:

- Avoid overprotecting your children.

- Encourage kids to reason and work out answers for themselves.

- Help kids reframe mistakes and deal with risks differently.

Avoid overprotecting kids

As a parent, you might worry about the kinds of danger your kids can be exposed to, and try to provide certainty in an attempt to keep them safe. This concern is understandable. It is important to protect young children from physical harm and to attend to their important needs. However, with older kids, and as kids grow up, the reality is that you will not be able to accommodate all their needs or eliminate all the risks. If you try to do so, there is a significant likelihood of diminishing your children's ability to be emotionally resilient and learn to cope with a range of situations – some of which you may not have encountered yourself when you were growing up. So you need to keep a healthy balance between keeping your kids safe and overprotecting them.

In fact, balance is a helpful approach to adopt when working with kids regardless of whether you are a parent or a clinician. Sometimes parents and therapists feel they have to teach kids how to be resilient. I take a different approach. In my counseling with Elizabeth, I offered her choices to manage her concerns grounded on the assumption that she could cope from the inside out. I just supported her while she tried out the various options – the idea of teaching kids to fish, rather than giving them the fish. This is a good antidote to overprotecting your child.

Encourage kids to reason and work out their own answers

A resilient kid is one who is able to reason and problem-solve across a range of situations. One of my biggest concerns when interacting with families is encountering parents who do the talking on behalf of kids who seem quite capable of speaking for themselves. For example, when I ask kids their opinions on what they would like to eat or do, I might get the father or mother answering on their behalf: "Oh, they do not like to eat that" or "they do not like to do that." I must confess that it takes a lot of restraint on my part to not blurt out my internal dialogue: "I am having a conversation with your kids. Can you please allow them to speak for themselves?"

I advise parents to stop hovering over their kids and piloting their worlds. For example, if you replace your kid's thinking for themselves with your own thinking, you run the risk of lessening your child's motivation to think critically, to tolerate not knowing, or to deal with uncertainties.

In this age of instant information, it is important for kids to develop the ability to reason for themselves. In so doing, they build the confidence to make informed decisions about what they read on the internet and to sort out different types of information and opinions.

You can nurture this discernment skill by allowing your kids to first come up with their own answers, as I have noted earlier.

You may worry about the kind of information your kid is able to access. You would be right in not allowing your child easy access to social media. I share similar beliefs. But for older kids who have to source information from the internet for their hobbies and projects, the question is more complicated. How do kids learn to differentiate legitimate information from misinformation?

A friend posed a question that I think reflects this kind of dilemma. "How do we let kids be kids in a world where they are constantly bombarded with information 24/7 from a young age?" she asked. "Unless we live in isolation, I do not know how this would play out practically. I am honestly curious about this."

My advice is to get to know your kids well and have an open dialogue with them. I often encourage my grandsons to ask questions on a range of topics, especially on their current interests, and I share with them my perspectives. The following are two examples of our discussions.

We were discussing different political and parliamentary systems.

"Why do we need a constitutional monarch in Australia?" Matthew asked.

"The monarch is a representative of the people, I replied. "If the government or other interest groups act against the will of the people, any citizen can write to the monarch directly and seek his or her help."

"So, the monarch is a protector of the people", Matthew said. "That's good."

In short, I tried to provide him with information about the role of the monarch, rather than giving him my opinion on whether a republic or a constitutional monarchy is right for Australia. In this way, I hoped that as he read more and became better informed, he could reason for himself the rights and wrongs of our political system.

We were discussing climate change and renewables. Nicholas had been researching the topic for his school.

"Nuclear seems like a good option," he said.

"How did you come to that conclusion?" I asked.

Nicholas proceeded to explain the pros and cons of each energy source.

You can have similar wide-ranging conversations with your kids and encourage them to think through the issues. I recommend employing the following strategies:

- Address their current interest and provide some facts for them to think about.
- Ask the "how" rather than the "why" questions in order to understand their reasoning.
- Consider what they already know about the subject matter, and what they have learned from the discussions.

When you build up your kids' confidence to think for themselves, you are reinforcing their self-belief that they will be able to use their power of reasoning to work through unfamiliar situations in future.

Help kids to reframe mistakes and deal with risks differently

Everyone makes mistakes. Kids need to be allowed to make mistakes, to encounter failures, and to experience the consequences of their failures. I have met many overprotective parents who try to ensure, for example, that their kids' school assignments are perfect. How can children learn from their mistakes or failures if they are not allowed to experience the consequences of their actions?

One way you can lessen your child's fears of making mistakes is to encourage them to accept and to reframe mistakes as learning opportunities. You could also encourage your kids to focus on their efforts, rather than just on the results. For example, you could ask: "What did you learn from your actions? How would you do it differently next time?" "Is there anything else that you could try in future?" When kids acknowledge that mistakes are something to learn from, rather than to avoid, they gain the confidence to adapt and to become more resilient.

Helping kids reframe mistakes.

What about coping with risks? I have known of anxious parents who tend to catastrophize danger and risks. I learned from my client Mark, who suffers from anxiety and panic attacks, that he was brought up by a highly anxious mother. His mother would constantly remind him of the accidents that might take place if he walked to school even with an older brother. "There are bad (or drunk) drivers on the road," his mother used to tell him. As a result, my client was chauffeured to school by his mother until he finished high school. Now, as a young man, he still constantly looks over his shoulder to ensure nothing bad ever happens. His anxiety translated into full-blown panic attacks when he had to travel for work. One of the insightful observations he made during counseling was: "My mother gave me love but she did not give me strength."

We need to be mindful not to pass on our anxiety to kids – the intergenerational legacy. Mark's mother could have said: "I am concerned about you crossing the road on your own. How about we learn to cross the road together, and I can teach you how to watch out for cars." Similarly, you can strengthen your kids' confidence by helping them learn practical skills, instead of overwhelming them with your fears.

In my counseling work with Mark, I tried to strengthen his resilience by encouraging him to accept that he is not a victim – that while he is the beneficiary of his mother's love, he does not need to be a beneficiary of her anxiety. I also helped him develop the emotional resilience and skills to tolerate and embrace his anxiety, rather than to be overwhelmed by it. Mark learned to reframe his fears differently:

I coped with my anxiety by just being mindful of any anxiety I have. Letting it come and letting it go. I realized that my tolerance to the anxiety underlines the problem. Previously I would say, "What if I won't be able to tolerate a panic attack?" Yesterday I was saying "I can tolerate it." Embracing my humanity and emotions. Just seeing them as an experience.[16]

Psychological Explanations and Key Learnings

In this chapter, I have shown from the stories of my clients, my mother and myself that a Spring kid is not defined by age, race, or culture. I highlighted how important being resilient is to kids' emotional development and personal growth. Resilience is intimately connected with feeling positive. When children feel they can cope and adapt to a range of situations and to life itself, they feel hopeful about their future. A sense of hardiness acquired from dealing with difficult or negative situations can help kids reframe mistakes and risks differently. This was the case with the clients I worked with.

You can play a key role in helping your child be more resilient. By not overprotecting them, but instead encouraging your kid to work out their own solutions, and to reframe mistakes and failures more positively, you can help strengthen your child's coping skills and sense of agency.

According to Clare Rowe, an Australian psychologist:

> Resilience is a skill that can be nurtured, and it's one of the most powerful protective factors against mental health issues. But resilience isn't built through therapy or education alone – it's built through life experiences. It's built by facing challenges, making mistakes, and learning from them. It's built by developing a sense of competence, mastery, and autonomy. We need to allow young people to experience failure, to struggle, and to solve their own problems. We need to provide them with support, but not always solutions. We need to model resilience ourselves, showing them that it's okay to face difficulties, and that they have the strength to overcome them.[17]

My mother's and my own experiences demonstrate that the attitude we adopt towards adversities and crises can make a significant difference. In Chinese, the word "crisis," *wei ji* (危 机),[18] comprises two words: *wei* meaning danger and *ji* meaning to arrive at a critical point in one's life where one could take a turn either for the better or for the worse. When my mother and I were confronted with consequential situations and experiences, we coped by not seeing ourselves as victims and drawing instead on our resilience to spring back.

Whenever I hear people say that life is hard, stressful and full of insurmountable challenges, I share with them my mother's life story. I appreciate that not everyone who encounters trauma or adverse events can surf life as spiritually as my mother did. However, I hope they will be inspired by her resilience to give the wave of life their best shot.

Helping your child cultivate being resilient is about helping them learn to work with negatives and positives. Each of us can either be a hero or a victim in our personal journeys. We have the capacity to be the authors and editors of our own lives. Helping your child learn to be resilient is not just a feel-good exercise; it is giving your child an invaluable asset for living a meaningful life.

Practice Guide

- Encourage your kids to look to inspiring individuals, including family members, for positive role-modeling.

- Be mindful that your interactions and communications with your children do not inhibit their capacity to be flexible and to adapt.

- Allow your children to make mistakes and to learn from those mistakes.

- Trust in your kids' ability to reason and to work out solutions for themselves.

- Encourage your kids to see themselves as agents of their own change, rather than as victims of their circumstances.

Chapter 4

IMAGINATIVE

Nurturing imagination for cognitive and social development

Let your child imagine and dream. It is priceless.

Playing with ants is not child's play

We were living in Singapore, where I practiced as a lawyer. As I arrived home from work one day, my frazzled babysitter rushed out, asking me to take my daughter Lynne away from the ants.

I raced to the apartment balcony. There I saw my 3-year-old daughter in deep concentration, watching a convoy of marching ants carrying leaves and twigs across the sand in the sandbox I had built for her on the balcony.

"Mum," Lynne asked, "where are the ants going? What are they carrying? Can I play with them?" I laughed at the spellbound wonder on Lynne's face as she followed the goings-on of the ants.

After reassuring the babysitter that the ants were harmless, I explained to Lynne: "They are building an ant nest. They are also looking for food. Would you like to help the ants?"

Lynne nodded her head enthusiastically. We went down to the garden, and collected leaves, twigs, and mud for the nest. I encouraged Lynne to use her imagination and allowed her to take the lead in building the nest. I watched in fascination as she constructed the nest and gave me a running commentary on her actions.

Lynne dug a shallow hole in the sand and filled it up with water.

"Making a water hole for ants," she said.

She paved the side of the waterhole with leaves.

"Making a garden for ants."

She used the twigs and leaves to make a shelter "from the sun and rain" for the ants. Then we sat quietly watching the ants crawling around their new home. Some ants fell into the water. Lynne looked worried. She put out her hand to rescue them. The ants bit her.

"Ouch! That hurts, Mum."

I explained that the ants were just protecting themselves, as they were afraid she might hurt them. Lynne kept quiet and thought for a while. She took a twig and placed it across the water hole, then floated some leaves in the water. She was pleased when some of the ants started to walk across the branch, while others used the leaves to cross the water.

"Mum, look, ants won't fall in the water now." Lynne smiled, clearly happy with her solutions. She used a twig to push the leaves with the ants on them along the water.

"Ants will not bite me now," she explained.

I was impressed with her understanding of the problem, and her problem-solving skills.

Lynne and I spent many happy hours that day, watching the ants. Each morning from then onwards, she would rush out to the sandbox and watch the ants scurrying around. Lynne took great delight in working on the nest, adding more leaves, twigs, and mud as needed.

To expand Lynne's interest in and knowledge about ants, I took her to a bookshop and encouraged her to choose some simple books about ants. We spent many more delightful hours learning about the different types of ants, their roles in the

"Mum, look, ants won't fall in the water now."

ant hierarchy, their habitats and food. We also learned that ants are highly sensitive to a change in the weather, and that they look for shelter if they sense rain coming.

"Mum, it's going to rain soon," Lynne said one day. "The ants are running for shelter."

And sure enough, the rain came pelting down soon after, as Lynne and I sat, reveling in our natural "ant weather gauge."

While our experiences with the ants took place many years ago, and Lynne is now herself the proud mother of two boys with whom I've also shared many wonderful experiences, I still recall our early learnings with fond memories. The ant story illustrates the many ways that being imaginative helps in the psychological, social, and creative development of kids.

As a caregiver, it is equally important for you to use your imagination, as your responses have a meaningful impact on your child's imagination. As I have shown in our encounter with the ants, it was our collaboration and role-playing that enabled Lynne and myself to learn from the ants and from each other.

In this chapter, I discuss the benefits of being imaginative and show how you can help your kids to cultivate this quality from a young age, through creative exercises and imaginative play.

What is being imaginative?

The fourth attribute of a Spring kid, being imaginative, benefits kids in many ways. At times, this creativity results in concrete, observable behaviors and at others in more subtle and indiscernible ones. These benefits include kids learning to:

- imagine possible worlds and work out alternative solutions
- experiment with and refine their problem-solving and conceptual skills
- understand their environment and experiences from fresh perspectives
- understand sophisticated concepts through role-playing
- master language and social and communication skills
- explore their internal worlds and express difficult emotions.

In this chapter, I showcase some activities you can use to stimulate your kids' creativity and imagination. It is essential that you make these activities fun and entertaining, and encourage your child to dream and make-believe naturally and freely.

Alison Gopnik,[19] a renowned American child psychologist, philosopher, and leading researcher in child development, has described children as the research and development division of adults. I believe that children are natural scientists and that their minds provide amazing laboratories for humanity. According to Gopnik, being imaginative requires us to consider and be open to a range of possibilities. Play in childhood is a good time for your kids to develop this ability, as it is during this period that they learn to move beyond their current experiences and imagine what is otherwise possible.

Imagining possible worlds

Philosophers and psychologists often talk about the mental process of imagining alternative worlds: the "What if" or "If only" kind of thinking about how things could have turned out differently had certain choices or decisions been made or not made. This kind of thinking is referred to as "counterfactual."

Until recently, child psychologists such as Jean Piaget theorized that young children are not capable of counterfactual thought, as this kind of thinking demands a highly developed ability to understand the relationship between current reality, outcomes, and alternatives. However, from her research, Gopnik observed that even young children are able to imagine possible worlds as alternatives to the one in which they currently live.

You may have watched with amusement as your children fashioned chairs and cushions into trains or airplanes to transport their toys to their holidays. Or when your kids dressed up to take their "child" to school. I was intrigued to witness this kind of counterfactual thinking in Lynne's problem-solving during her encounter with the ants. She was able to make the causal connection between the ants falling into the water, her being bitten when she tried to help them, and her needing to work out other alternative solutions. So, she reimagined a twig into a bridge, the leaves into rafts, and another twig as a pole to push the leaves along.

When you give young kids the freedom to use their imagination to generate other possibilities, you are helping them think outside the box and to come up with innovative ideas that sometimes you might have taken for granted. Children often come up with unusual answers because their minds are not constrained by what has been or what should be, but are energized instead by what could be. The ability to think creatively augurs well for kids in the future, when they will have to face and overcome unfamiliar challenges.

Understanding sophisticated concepts through role-play

As children grow up, their counterfactual thinking becomes more complex and intriguing as their imagined worlds become more sophisticated, and they fantasize about becoming wizards, astronauts, or superheroes. You can encourage your kids to use their imaginations by creating scenarios involving sophisticated concepts and role-playing, as my experience with my grandsons demonstrates.

When Matthew and Nicholas were 6 and 3 years old respectively, we discussed nationality and citizenship. The boys wanted to know more about the two concepts. Matthew was born in the United States, while Nicholas was born in Australia. Both boys have dual American-Australian citizenships, being born to American and Australian parents.

"Why are we both Americans and Australians?" they asked. "Can we become an American president or an Australian prime minister?"

Briefly, nationality is conferred by the country of birth, while citizenship is conferred by a country in which one is born or resides.[20] An American president must be a natural-born citizen of the United States and can hold dual citizenships. On the other hand, an Australian prime minister must be an Australian citizen. They are unable to hold dual citizenships, and so those with two must renounce one citizenship and retain only the Australian one.

While I was impressed with my grandsons' interest, and piqued by their questions, I was at a loss as to how to explain such complex concepts in an accessible way.

"Matthew," I said, "you could become an American president. An American president has to be born in the USA, and you were born there. You could also become an Australian prime minster as you have an Australian citizenship. However, to be an Australian prime minister, you would have to give up your American citizenship. Australia does not allow its prime ministers to have two citizenships.

"Nicholas, you cannot become an American president, as you were not born there. However, you can become an Australian prime minister if you give up your American citizenship."

"Cool!" Matthew and Nicholas said. "We understand."

I looked at them with some doubt as to whether they did understand. I had not counted on their comprehension ability, imagination, and sense of humor, as their role-playing showed.

Matthew put out his hand.

"Hello, I'm President Matthew. Nice to meet you."

"Hello, President Matthew," Nicholas replied. "I'm Prime Minister Nicholas. "Welcome to Australia. Would you like a barbie?"

"I am a president. I do not play with barbie dolls." Matthew pretended to look offended.

"'Barbie' is what we call barbecue in Australia. That is how we cook our meat." Nicholas roared with laughter.

They proceeded to take out their toy plates, forks, and plastic meat. They built an imaginary fire, barbecued the steaks, and ate them with pretend gusto.

"I'm President Matthew."
"I'm Prime Minister Nicholas. Have a Barbie!"

To this day, I still chuckle at the memory of how well my grandsons understood the differences between nationality and citizenship, and were able to use language, humor, and counterfactual thinking to enact an amusing exchange between two fictional world leaders. Their role-play shows that kids are never too young to be interested in and to engage with big questions or subtle ideas.

Encourage your kids to wonder about the world and about life. Ask them open-ended questions; for example, "How would you describe a dog to a person from the moon?" or "What made you smile today?" Let them use their imagination to demonstrate their answers to your questions. You can play along with whatever scenario your kids create, so they are inspired to push the limits of their imagination.

Ideas to inspire kids' imagination and help them explore their inner worlds

There are myriad ways to boost and strengthen your kids' imagination. These activities include drawing, painting, role-playing, dressing-up, storytelling, reading, problem-solving, and using stimulating material for experimentation. The list is endless and limited only by your and your child's imagination.

When you offer your child a gadget to play with, ask yourself: "Is the play in the gadget or is the play in the child?" If the play is in the gadget – for example, with battery-operated toys – kids will soon tire of them, as these toys leave nothing much to the imagination. However, if the play is in the child – for example, with freeform items – children will be endlessly entertained as they imagine all the possibilities they can create with the device or material.

Using drawing and sketches

One of my favorite creative ideas is the use of drawings and sketches. I employ this exercise regularly with my grandsons, other kids, and my young clients. The following are some instructive examples for you to consider.

Can you design my house?

A few years ago, Matthew signed up for a holiday architectural design course. Coincidentally, I was building my own house. I teased him about designing my house. He came up with this interesting concept. Matthew's recommendation was to build a marine-inspired metabolism

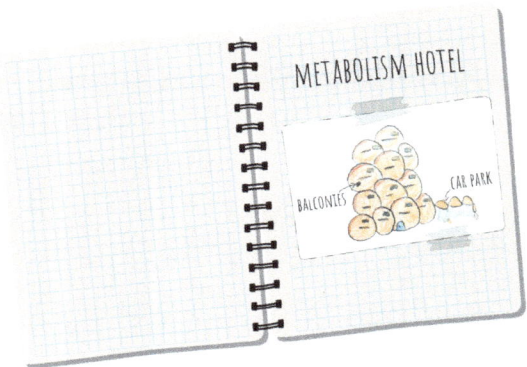

Matthew's metabolism hotel.

hotel on the land. He designed a hotel clad with fish scales as balconies and corals for the parking lot. The blue front door represents the ocean. I shared Matthew's design with my architect Pierre. "It's amazing what kids can do free of council regulations and other technicalities," Pierre remarked.

Similarly, you can involve your kids by inviting them to participate in your current projects, for example building a tree house, constructing a fishpond or designing a garden. Try to incorporate some of their ideas and suggestions wherever possible, to motivate them to continue their participation.

Helping kids express their feelings through drawings

When I work with kids in therapy, one of the challenges is helping them to get in touch with how they feel, and to describe and share their emotions. Clinicians and parents often encounter the same difficulties.

Encouraging younger kids to draw is one of the most effective means of helping children express their feelings. This was the approach I used with Shauna, a 6-year-old client who was caught in a very difficult marital dispute between her combative parents.

Shauna was an only child, and both parents wanted sole custody of her. However, her father was often depressed and unable to provide her with the emotional stability she needed, as he was struggling with his own issues. Meanwhile, her mother, a vivacious professional, often spent evenings away from home, returning only after Shauna and her father were asleep.

During my counseling with Shauna, she indicated that she did not like her mother going out so often. She was however not forthcoming when I asked her how she felt. She looked down and bit her lips, as if to stop herself from saying anything disloyal to either parent. I opted for another approach, and gave her a sheet of paper and a box of crayons.

"Shauna, can you draw a picture of when Mummy gets ready to go out?" I asked. What do you do?"

With deep concentration, she sketched a giant toy hippopotamus, which had been a present from her father when she was 3 years old. Shauna drew herself sitting in the arms of the purple hippo for comfort and security. In front of the hippo, she drew two beautiful red high-heeled shoes. Then she drew herself kissing one shoe. She drew large tears running down her face.

It was a poignant picture of a desolate child. My heart went out to her, but I did not offer any comments.

"Shauna, would you like to tell me about your drawing? Who is hippo?"

"Hippo is my friend, Hippy. Daddy gave her to me for my birthday. Before Mummy and Daddy fought a lot."

"What do you do with Hippy?" I asked.

"I sit with Hippy and eat with Hippy. I read with Hippy and sleep with her when Daddy and Mummy go to bed. Hippy looks after me when I feel sad." Shauna cried quietly.

"When do you feel sad?" I added.

"When Mummy goes out, and Daddy goes to sleep. I feel lonely and afraid. No one plays with me except Hippy. I hug Hippy to sleep."

"Can you tell me about the red shoes in your drawing?"

"They are Mummy's going-out shoes. She has lots of shoes. When she takes out the shoes, I know she is going out again. I asked her not to go. But she doesn't listen. When she goes out, I take another pair of red shoes from her cupboard and put them beside me and Hippy. I pretend that Mummy is still there in the room with us. I take one of her shoes and kiss them. I pretend that Mummy kisses me back." Shauna is crying openly now. I allowed her to sob.

"How do you feel, Shauna?" I asked.

"I feel very sad," Shauna replied quietly. "It hurts a lot here [she pointed to her heart and her rib cage]. I'm feeling angry. I don't want Mummy and Daddy to fight. I don't want Mummy to go out all the time. I don't want Daddy to sleep all the time. I'm only 6 years old."

Later, I shared Shauna's drawing and explanations with her parents.

"Hippy is my friend when Mummy goes out at night."

They were deeply saddened to learn about her emotional world from her drawing, and how lonely and afraid she felt. They were also remorseful about how they had forgotten about her pain in the midst of their own.

Her parents still went through with the divorce. However, they fought less over her, agreed to joint custody and made significant efforts to spend time with her when the other parent was absent. Her mother reduced her outings, and her father stayed up until Shauna fell asleep.

Shauna never got the "happy family" she dreamed of. Nevertheless, by disclosing her real feelings through her drawing, she was able to motivate her parents to moderate their behaviors and offer her some much-needed emotional security. The extent of Shauna's visual expressions and undirected explanations of her drawing showed the voiceless depth of her pain and suffering.

You can adapt my approach to encourage your kids to draw their interior worlds and help them express deep-seated emotions when words are not easily available to them. Make sure you allow your kids to illustrate their interior worlds freely, and listen to their explanations unimpeded by any preconceived assumptions and conclusions. If you are planning to share your child's drawing with others, get your child's permission to do so, as they need to feel you can be trusted with what they have disclosed.

Being imaginative: Adult role-play

As I noted earlier, parents play a crucial role in fostering children's imagination and creativity. Your role-playing can often kick-start your kids' imagination and encourage them to think outside the box.

The experience of Gerald, an 8-year-old boy, and his father Michael, whom I was counseling, illustrates this complementary relationship well.

"Helping your kid run away from home"

Gerald was headstrong and tended to act defiantly when he felt his parents Michael and Michelle did not understand or agree to his demands. His default reaction was to "run away" from home. He would stuff his backpack with his pajamas and favorite Lego toy, grab his security blanket and walk out of the front door, closing it with a loud bang to let his parents know he was going. His parents would usually panic and end up locking the door, giving in to his demands or turning on the television to distract him.

During one of our counseling sessions, his parents explained that they were at a loss as to how to moderate his defiant behavior.

"Use your imagination. Help him run away from home," I suggested. "Every time Gerald doesn't get his way, he reacts by running away from home. And then you respond by panicking and stopping his actions. Ironically, you are enabling the very behavior you wish to stop. Gerald doesn't have to learn to modify his behavior because he has his parents to do that for him. Gerald needs to experience the consequences of his behavior himself and be motivated to change it. So, I would encourage you to use your imagination and creativity to see how you can help him do that."

Michael and Michelle took my suggestions on board. At the next counseling session, Michael reported that Gerald had tried to run away from home again, as he had done many times before.

"I thought about what you recommended," Michael said. "To use my imagination and creativity to change his behavior. Last week when he walked out of the door, we decided to let him go. I got into my car and started to follow him. I saw him walking along the pavement. I stopped and asked him whether he wanted a ride. Gerald looked at me with surprise. I said, 'I'm going to check you into the hotel down the road. If you are going to run away from home, you might as well be comfortable and sleep in a hotel.'"

"What happened then?" I asked.

"Gerald was taken aback," Michael replied. "He said, 'You and Mummy are not going to stop me from running away? You are just going to let me go?' I said to Gerald, 'Yes, if you really want to. It's your choice. Call us when

**"I am going to check you into
a hotel down the road."**

you want to come home.' Gerald kept quiet for a moment, and then he said, 'Well if you and Mummy are not going to stop me, I won't run away. I will just go home and watch television. Can we go home now?'"

Michael said he had found it hard to stifle his laughter. He was delighted his creative solutions seemed to work. I smiled, equally impressed with Michael's creativity. "Well done, Michael," I said.

Gerald has learned the meaning of the expression, "Be careful what you wish for." The exchange with his father showed that when Gerald experienced the consequences of his behavior and realized that his actions no longer pushed his parents' buttons, or got him the reactions he was hoping for, he stopped running away. Michael said that now when Gerald demanded something and his parents did not agree, he no longer tried to run away. Instead, he asked his parents, "Why can't I do that?" The family would then sit down and have a sensible discussion.

This vignette shows how you can use your own creativity to negotiate with your child in an innovative way. When you facilitate your kids to contemplate the imagined outcomes – good, bad, or neutral – of their own behavior, they learn to make appropriate decisions. By employing counterfactual thinking, Michael was able to let Gerald picture a possible world in which he got his wish to run away from home but had to stay in a hotel by himself. Gerald's decision not to proceed showed he recognized that this imaginary scenario was not a comfortable outcome for him.

Psychological Explanations and Key Learnings

Children need to dream and create. It is how they grow. Imaginative activities are not just child's play. While these activities give children hours of fun, the real benefits of such pursuits are to help the development of the child's psychological, emotional, and cognitive skills across a range of situations. I have shown how you can use the exercises to help your kids solve problems, develop critical thinking, learn from their mistakes, master social and communication skills, and express difficult emotions.

To help your kids expand their imagination, encourage them to use counterfactual thinking – the ability to imagine different possibilities – and help them use these possibilities to modify their current experiences. And finally, you can use your own creativity to work alongside your child and offer alternative solutions for your child to ponder.

Practice Guide

- Support your kids' current interests and engage with them with an open mind in order to understand their thinking from their perspectives.

- Allow your children to make and learn from their mistakes without your intervention. Ask open-ended questions about their rationale and motivation.

- Introduce your kids to a range of activities and materials to inspire their imagination and creativity. Keep the material simple and freeform.

- Use your own imagination and creativity to role-model and to provide the scaffolding for your children's ideas.

Chapter 5

NIMBLE

Fostering adaptability, creativity and responsiveness

"Cherry blossoms teach us to be nimble, to flower, and to let go. I like the meaning of my name."

– Sakura

Nimbleness, the fourth attribute of the term "SPRING," speaks to both physical and mental qualities. The physical aspect of being nimble embodies the quality of being quick and light in movement, moving with ease and agility. The mental qualities of being nimble involve quick thinking and being witty, flexible, and adaptable.

It is important to help kids develop both physical and mental nimbleness. This is crucial to their psychological development, and to your raising emotionally healthy kids. In this chapter, I focus on the mental qualities of nimbleness and recommend some exercises to enhance this dimension.

Being nimble

The most essential qualities of being nimble are adaptability and agility. When you show your kids how to adapt and respond to changing circumstances, you are helping them cultivate the skill of what I call "respond-ability". The concept of respond-ability refers to the ability to respond mindfully and intuitively to each unique situation. With respond-ability, we learn to let go of habitual responses and thoughts about "What should be," or "What is in it for me," and respond to what is needed.[21] A simple example of respond-ability is when we encounter an elderly person struggling to cross the road and rush out to help spontaneously.

By helping your children to be nimble, you are also supporting them to lay the foundation for being spiritual, positive, resilient, and imaginative, the attributes I discussed in Chapters 1–4. Mental nimbleness enables your kids to develop quick thinking and the agility of mind to:

- adapt and respond to changing circumstances
- communicate through stories, wit, and humor
- understand different perspectives through role-playing
- problem-solve through analysis, strategy, and improvisation
- develop discipline, responsibility, and respect.

It is important that you help your kids be nimble from a young age by encouraging them to develop all these qualities concurrently. The following are examples of some supportive exercises and practices.

Adaptability: Lessons from nature

One of the most inspiring ways you can help your children learn to adapt is to let them experience adaptability in nature. An example is my nature walk with my "friend" Sakura.

A spiritual encounter with cherry blossoms

It is mid-August in Sydney – still officially winter in the southern hemisphere. This year, however, spring seems to have come early, as evidenced by the flowering trees. One beautiful morning I take a walk with my imaginary friend Sakura (named after the Japanese word for cherry blossom).

In quiet reflection, we watch the rows of cherry blossom trees lining the park and filling the air with their subtle perfume.

"I thought cherry blossoms flower in spring," Sakura says.

"You're right," I reply. "However, this autumn [fall], the weather has been wet and warm. Nature is nimble and adaptable. Nature doesn't observe a chronological clock. Instead, the seasons follow their own rhythm, and when the conditions are right, spring arrives. At such time, the trees just respond and the flowers bloom."

"They are so beautiful," Sakura says.

"Cherry blossoms teach us how to adapt and to let go. I like the meaning of my name."

– Sakura

"Yes they are. Let's welcome them like guests arriving unexpectedly and early. Let's embrace them with open arms and enjoy what nature has given us in friendship.

"Nature also teaches us another important lesson about living. In Japan, your name, Sakura, symbolizes a time of renewal and growth. However, as cherry blossoms flower for only a short time, they also teach us to understand and accept change and impermanence.

> That means we learn to enjoy everything and everyone when they're with us, and to let them go when they are no longer there."
>
> "So cherry blossoms teach us to be nimble, to flower, and to let go," Sakura replies. "I like the meaning of my name. That's so special."
>
> Sakura and I walk home happily holding hands.

You can share my encounter with the cherry blossoms with your kids to demonstrate how they can practice respond-ability by being mindful of what is happening now. Encourage your children to adapt by introducing them to similar happenings in nature; for example, the transformation of a caterpillar into a butterfly, the opening of new leaves on a "winter-lifeless" branch, or the building of nests by birds in readiness for the birth of their fledglings as soon as the weather warms up.

Being nimble and learning to respond to change are major themes in the account by Her Royal Highness Catherine The Princess of Wales of her experience with cancer. Catherine was diagnosed with cancer in early 2024 and spoke about her medical experience, and the lessons she learned about life, in a video she posted in September that year.[22] Catherine said she learned that life is fragile and changeable, and that when one is confronted with mortality, it brings a sense of humility and a fresh way of looking at everything. She shared that she and Prince William are thankful for simple things, like loving and being loved. Catherine added that she continues her recovery with a sense of renewed hope and a deep gratitude for life.

Catherine recorded her video in the woods of her Norfolk home. Nature appeared to have given her and her family great solace, comfort, and a sense of renewal. Her poignant sharing of the uncertainty of life, of focusing on what is important, of adapting and cultivating a new outlook on life are valuable lessons you can share with your children about how to navigate unforeseen life events. I admire her meditative attitude and wish her well in this transformative chapter of her life.

Effective communication using stories, wit, and humor

Kids love a good story and storytelling. They also love a good laugh. The things that kids find funny reflect a high level of thinking and what is currently taking place in their minds. You can use your children's love of stories and their sense of humor to help them to enhance their mental nimbleness. As I've described in the earlier chapters of this book, I often use stories and humor with my grandsons to help them develop their mental acuity.

Learning through reading and telling stories

As a young child, my grandson Matthew loved Mem Fox's Where is the Green Sheep?[23] The book tells a delightful, humorous story of encountering different kinds of sheep in the countryside, except for the green one. Fox invited her readers to join her in looking for the missing sheep. Matthew loved the drama, the humor, the rhythm of the words, and the beautiful illustrations. He asked me to read him the book many, many times.

When he was 4 years old, I suggested to Matthew that he might like to write his own version of the green sheep book. Matthew wrote a play, which he dictated to me, called the "Angelina and Alice cow story." His play tells of a white cow searching for a purple leaf with the help of his friend, a purple sheep. The leaf was hidden in Field Number 10. The cow could not count but was afraid to tell Sheep this, until Sheep encouraged him to tell the truth and assured him he would not be judged.

Once upon a time, white cow and purple sheep were looking for the purple leaf.

When they found the leaf, Cow ate it, not realizing the leaf had magical powers and that it would make him grow. Cow grew as tall as the beanstalk and floated into the sky. Sheep was concerned about his safety. She managed to round up thousands of sheep and lassoed Cow back to his original size.

Matthew and I decided to perform the play to the family. At the performance, Matthew explained that his play comprised of four main characters: Angelina, Alice, the white cow, and the purple sheep. Matthew announced that he would play Angelina, who would in turn play the role of the purple sheep, and I would play Alice, who would in turn act the part of the white cow. The following is an extract from Matthew's story.

Cow grew as tall as a beanstalk in the sky.

Storyteller: Angelina and Alice walked and walked until they found a piece of paper lying on the ground. The paper said, "Head north for the purple leaf today."

Alice: Angelina, what number field is the leaf growing in?

Angelina: Field Number 10. We can ask White Cow to come with us if he can count. Cow, can you count?

Cow: Of course, I can count [He really cannot count or read, but he is too shy to tell them].

Storyteller: The cow disappeared. He is supposed to tell the truth, and when he does not tell the truth, he disappears, and his friends cannot see him until he tells the truth.

Sheep: Cow, it is alright to tell the truth. Don't be embarrassed. It is okay. You will be fine. If you can't count, you should tell people the truth. That is what a good cow would do because you are a very smart cow. You will always be my friend.

Cow: Thank you. Well, to tell you the truth, I can't count.

Sheep: Don't worry. You can tell us because we are your friends. And friends forgive friends. Especially when they are scared to do something.

Storyteller: Purple Sheep and White Cow found the purple leaf, which is magical. When the cow ate it, he grew and grew until he became the tallest cow ever.

Cow: Grow, grow. [He didn't know that the leaf was magical. And he became as tall as a beanstalk.]

Sheep: Why are you up in the sky, Cow?

Cow: Because I said, "Grow, grow" when I ate the purple leaf. And it made me grow this tall.

Sheep: I need to get help from all the other sheep I can find. This is an emergency.

Storyteller: Purple Sheep ran to look for the other sheep. She found thousands of them. Together, they made a lasso and pulled cow back to its original size.

Matthew appeared to understand the multiple layers of role-playing, for example writing about an individual who plays a character, and the character in turn playing another character

(Matthew playing Angelina who plays the white cow), and fleshing out the personalities of their assumed characters. According to Alison Gopnik, the ability of a child to understand different perspectives from diverse imaginary identities demonstrates how young minds are able to reflect individually and interactively.

Matthew's script showed that he understood the essence of the green sheep story. He was able to communicate the main theme – the search for a green sheep – and substitute that with the search for a purple leaf. He also incorporated humor and drama in his story, describing how White Cow ate the magic purple leaf and grew as tall as a beanstalk, floating into the sky, so that Purple Sheep then needed to get urgent help from thousands of sheep to rescue the cow.

Some compelling themes in Matthew's writing revolved around ethics, empathy, and morality. Matthew emphasized the importance of White Cow telling the truth about not being able to count, and of Purple Sheep empathizing with White Cow when he finally told the truth, reassuring him that all was forgiven. These themes suggest kids have an intuitive sense of ethics, empathy, and morality. As Alison Gopnik noted, children are possessed of the foundation of morality from a young age. Matthew is now 14 years old. When I recently shared the script with him, he laughed, replying: "I didn't know I could think like that. That is so funny." He obviously still has a sense of humor.

Help your child to cultivate perspective-taking through stories, either the ones you share with them or those you encourage them to make up. Encourage your children to role-play their narratives and explain to you the rationale of their stories. That way, you will get a better understanding of how your child understands ethics, morality, and other positive values. It also helps if you act the part of one of the imagined characters, and encourage the family to dress up for the roles as well.

Using humor and wit

One of the most effective and fun ways for you to promote mental agility in your kids is through the use of humor. Foster a love of jokes in them, as banter and witty exchanges provide excellent training for quick thinking. Let me share some examples of the exercises I enjoy with my grandsons.

From a young age, Matthew and Nicholas have shown an inclination towards quirky humor. Our trips to bookshops often see us browsing in the funny books section. Their birthday wishes are often for another joke book, and one of our favorite car ride activities is the "Knock, knock" game. We try to make our questions as silly and as ironic as possible, so the answers are always entertaining. One of the jokes I love goes:

Knock, knock.

Who's there?

Somebody.

Somebody who?

Somebody who can't reach the doorbell! [huge laughter].

When Matthew was 10 and Nicholas was 6 years old, I challenged them to a funny game using the internet. The idea was to search for hilarious answers to our open-ended questions. The following are some samples of this exercise, which you can adapt and play with your own young family members. Make the questions as outlandish or as quirky as each of you can dream up.

The internet humor game

Belinda: My question is, "What do you want to be?" Search the internet and show us your answers in pictures. The answers can be as silly as you make them.

Nicholas: "I want to be a banana."

Matthew: "I want to be annoying like Nai-Nai."

Belinda: "I want to eat my grandsons for lunch."

"I want to be a banana!"   "I want to be annoying like Nai-Nai!"   "I want to eat my grandsons for lunch!"

Matthew: My question is, "Find the funniest image you can." My image is "Fish bullying dog."

Nicholas: My image is "Looking for Matthew's missing brain."

Belinda: My image is "Grandma is a ninja."

"Fish bullying a dog."   "Nobody move! I'm looking for Matthew's missing brain!"   "Grandma is a ninja."

Help your kids communicate easily through storytelling, humorous vignettes, and jokes. Introduce a touch of the absurd in the games you play with them and encourage them to give nonsensical answers so that they learn to appreciate the funny side of things. Allow your children the freedom to think creatively. In so doing, you might be surprised at how nimble their imaginations are. They might even surpass your own, as I discovered during the internet humor game.

Problem-solving skills: Analyze, strategize, improvise

One of the important benefits of kids being nimble is their agility in problem-solving. To work out solutions in a timely manner, kids need to be able to analyze, strategize, and improvise. They also need to cultivate the discipline to focus and sustain their attention on the activities.

Depending on the age of your child, exercises that are helpful in developing critical thinking include games such as draughts, chess, Minecraft, puzzles, scrabbles, Lego, and sudoku. Moreover, when kids are involved with their games, they build up their ability to concentrate and complete the task. Learning a musical instrument is another excellent practice to build mental discipline and concentration.

In the following example, I discuss how playing chess helps enhance kids' problem-solving skills. Many of the principles of playing chess are applicable to the other games and crafts I have suggested.

"We won. We won. Let's do it again!"

Over the years, I have enjoyed playing all kinds of chess games with Matthew and Nicholas: English chess, Chinese chess and the Japanese game of Go, which, given the different kind of rules associated with each game, call for varying analytical and strategizing skills. I also encourage my grandsons to play as a pair against me, so they learn to make crucial decisions as a team. The following picture shows the excitement on the faces of Matthew (aged 7) and Nicholas (aged 4) when they won their chess game on an extra-large chess board.

Exercises using board games do not need to be expensive, as such games allow for much improvisation. For example, you can draw a chess board using chalk on the driveway and stones, rocks, and leaves as chess pieces. The potential for creative variation is endless. Allow your child to choose the substitute material.

Being nimble: Developing discipline, responsibility, and respect

Play can also serve as a helpful means for kids to learn discipline, responsibility, and respect. You can foster these qualities through the simple act of getting the kids to help you put away their play items. At the end of a chess game, for example, I assign Matthew and Nicholas the task of checking that all the pieces are accounted for (this exercise also helps them with

Books are our friends. Please take care of them.

counting skills). I encourage them to replace any missing or broken chess piece with painted bottle caps, Lego pieces, or any craft material that is available. Together, we store the chess pieces neatly in the box, ready for the chess set to be used again next time.

Another simple and fun way for you to help your kids to learn discipline, responsibility, and respect is to allow them to set up a kids' reading center. For this exercise, I recommend you work with your children to devise a simple classification system; for example sorting out the books according to colors, subject matters, book sizes, or author names. The kids can also work out the rules for the reading center: borrowing hours, a sign to maintain silence, and an inspirational quote such as "Books are our friends. Please take care of them." At the end of each reading session, assign each child the responsibility of putting away the books, following the agreed classification. Older kids can help design a "borrowing card," which family members can sign for the book they take out and agree to return within the prescribed time. Token "penalties" for late returns can be decided by the kids themselves.

You will be amazed at how much learning and critical thinking your kids develop from this simple exercise, especially in designing their own classification system. They will also develop respect and care for their toys and books when they take responsibility for the play items instead of expecting you to do so on their behalf. I have used similar exercises when my daughter was young. I am happy to share that most of her toys, board games, and books are fairly intact and still used by Matthew and Nicholas today. Anyone who constantly had to tell kids to put away their play items and books will appreciate that the time invested in these acts of care and responsibility is well spent.

Psychological Explanations and Key Learnings

The components of being nimble – such as adaptability, quick thinking, humor, ethics, morality, responsibility, and respect – help kids to cultivate important psychological, emotional, and social skills. Kids learn best when they are not consciously learning and the exercises are not perceived as homework or chores. The activities I recommend can be implemented easily and inexpensively, as they can be generated from what is available in nature, your everyday surrounds, and the kids' own trove of toys, board games, and books.

The most essential ingredient is your role. It means setting aside some emotional time and space for you to be present with your kids when you are engaged in the activities. At such times, my advice is to turn off your phone and your computer. Enjoy this time with your kids, learn and laugh together. I know I have learned and laughed a lot when I was "playing" with Sakura, Matthew, and Nicholas. Time spent in this manner is priceless.

Practice Guide

- Introduce your kids to a range of activities and experiences to strengthen their nimbleness. Keep the activities simple and fun.

- Incorporate humor and fun into the exercises. Allow the activities to be as silly and funny as possible.

- Use your kids' current resources such as toys, games, and books for the exercises.

- Allow your children to take the lead in the role-playing and activities.

Chapter 6

GRATEFUL

Strengthening respect, appreciation,
empathy and compassion

"A grateful heart turns what we have into enough."

– Venerable Dr. K. S. Dhammaratana

Being grateful, the sixth and final attribute in the term "SPRING," is the jewel in the crown. The capacity to be grateful, feel grateful, and express gratitude is one of the most valuable qualities of being human. In this chapter, I explore what it means to be grateful, from a general perspective and from my personal experiences.

Gratitude is like a tapestry. Every thread that is woven into the design contributes to the overall beauty and strength of the finished rug. Like a tapestry, when a child's development is strengthened by the quality threads of SPRING, the child grows up with a life laced with grace. love, and kindness.

Being grateful

Encouraging your kids to be grateful involves you helping them to embrace an attitude and a mindset that appreciate the gifts and blessings in their lives, big and small. Raising grateful kids is a process, not a goal, and small steps can bring about immeasurable change. According to Becky Kennedy,[24] an American clinical psychologist, gratitude is a feeling rather than a behavior. Kids who feel grateful tend to respond and act with gratitude.

Gratitude to an unknown taxi driver

When we are touched by an act of kindness, especially when the deed is unexpected and spontaneous, the sense of gratitude feels like a gentle wave cascading over us in moments of quiet reflection. Such was my memory of my encounter with a kind taxi driver 15 years ago.

One very hot day during a visit to Singapore, I was standing by the curbside waiting for a taxi. I was exhausted, but was unable to flag down a taxi as there was a change of shift. A few minutes later a taxi crossed the road, stopped, and offered me a ride, which I gratefully accepted. The driver explained that he was going to his Friday prayers at his local mosque and was running late.

"Why did you stop for me then?" I asked.

He explained, "I am a Muslim. I follow the teachings of Islam. Islam teaches us to practice compassion."

"I saw a human being in need. One day, you will do the same for another human being."

When I arrived at my hotel, I offered to pay him but he declined.

"A good deed is given with a good heart," he said. "We cannot take payment for doing the right thing. All religions are the same. They teach kindness and compassion. And helping when we see a need. You were limping and looking very tired. I saw a human being in need. I don't need compensation for being kind. It is who I am. One day, you will do the same for another human being."

I was so touched, I nearly cried.

Recently, I posted about the incident on my law alumni group chat. I was pleasantly surprised by the responses I received.

"A heartwarming and wonderous experience of the humaneness of mankind," one classmate wrote.

"I agree," I replied. "That's why after so many years I am still choked up when I recall the experience."

A second classmate posted: "I am choked up reading this on a Friday. God bless you for sharing. God bless the good Samaritan."

Another classmate who was moved by the story forwarded the post to her network in Singapore and Malaysia, where it went viral. She shared a reply from one of her friends: "This is such a special thing that happened. Healing and soothing. All Singaporeans and Malaysians should know about the kind driver."

I was glad the story touched so many hearts, as it did mine. After my encounter, I tried to look for the taxi driver to thank him properly. However, I was not able to do so as I did not have his name or his taxi number. So I thought I would honor his act of kindness by writing about it in this book.

Even though the encounter took place so many years ago, I have never forgotten that act of generosity and remain grateful to this day. I recount this story here as the taxi driver's actions illustrated many of the qualities of a Spring kid, regardless of age, gender or religion. He:

- was mindful of my pain and empathized with the suffering of a fellow human being

- was authentic in his practice of the teachings of Islam, showing kindness and compassion, and forsaking monetary rewards for his actions

- demonstrated a sense of respond-ability in exercising an appropriate response to a unique situation could see the interconnectedness of everything – "One day, you will do the same for another human being."

What moved me most was the knowledge that my classmates, regardless of which religion they practice (and some are atheists), were all profoundly touched when they read about human kindness. Nowadays, whenever people talk about the negativity of different religions, I share with them my experience, the essence of which is that an unknown taxi driver taught me the purest act of humanness comes from the heart, rather than from the mind. The simple thought I wish to share about my experience with the taxi driver is this: In the midst of the endless negative news we read on social and print media, wouldn't it be wonderful if the media strived to report acts of kindness, thoughtfulness, and compassion in their programs each day?

Why does being grateful matter?

It is important to raise kids who practice gratitude from a young age. Grateful kids experience better mental health, as they feel psychologically, emotionally, and socially more connected with themselves and with others. They also develop greater resilience, as they often appreciate what they have. More importantly, practicing gratefulness matters for kids because the practice helps reduce their sense of entitlement and need for instant gratification, the bane of most parents and of contemporary society.

When an infant cries, they are asking for food or comfort. However, when a child reaches the age of 4 or 5, many parents would be familiar with the constant refrain of "Can I have that?" or "I want it now!" The endless requests for new toys, chocolates, and the like may follow when parents take their kids to the shops. This demand for instant gratification, often reinforced by parental practices, social media, and the internet, can result in a sense of entitlement: "I want it all and all at the same time," or what I call a "me first" attitude.

Instant gratification and a sense of entitlement cut across all ages, generations, and spectrums of society. You may be familiar with some of the following scenarios:

- Children who constantly get their way may start to believe they are special and that the world revolves around their wants and desires. While kids usually outgrow this sense of entitlement, sometimes they do not. You may have encountered adults who still behave like 6-year-old children.

- The internet promoting the ease of "buy now, pay later" schemes and online shopping means that anyone can satisfy their purchasing habits with one click of the mouse. I recall a client telling me how worried she was when she came home from work to find her 10-year daughter using her credit card to purchase a toy online. My client said her daughter told her, "Mummy, I have to get that toy NOW. I cannot wait until my birthday to get it."

- Retailers and organizations taking advantage of the need for instant gratification by offering same-day delivery services or streaming full seasons of television shows instead of making them available over several months.

Demands for immediate outcomes have consequences beyond internet usage and purchasing habits. Kids who are unable to wait to gratify their needs will not develop the ability to tolerate boundaries and restraint. When these needs are not fulfilled, the psychological reactions are usually one of anxiety, tension, frustration, and stress. If children are brought up with a 'me first" mindset, it is hardly surprising that they grow up not feeling grateful for what they already have. As Becky Kennedy explained, gratitude is not the absence of frustration and disappointment. It is about learning to manage frustration and disappointment through perspective-taking and appreciation.

Differentiating between wants and needs

How can you help your child deal with frustration and disappointment arising from the fear of missing out? One helpful approach is to help your child differentiate between wants and needs. I learned this valuable distinction at my first meditation retreat many years ago.

At the retreat, we were encouraged to eat only one meal a day, in keeping with the tradition of my meditation teachers, a Buddhist monk and a nun. All the attendees loaded up their plates. My own plate was overflowing. I was worried I was going to get hungry later if I did not fill up now.

At lunch, my meditation teacher asked us to reflect and thank the volunteers who run the retreat and cooked the meals. My teacher also announced that we had to eat everything on our plates.

"But there is so much on my plate. I can't finish it all!" I exclaimed.

"All of you have to eat what you put on your plates as you appear to be more concerned about what you want rather than what you need," my teacher replied.

For the rest of the retreat, I filled my plate with only what I needed. And I never went hungry even once.

I took away two important lessons from that retreat:

- Being grateful is grounded on an awareness and appreciation of how many people were involved, or how things were put in place, for us to enjoy the activities. This helps create a sense of thankfulness to the individuals who have lent a hand.

- Differentiate between wants and needs. When we exercise the discipline and responsibility to put on our plates only the amount of food we require, we become mindful that what we want usually exceeds what we really need.

I have never forgotten these insights. You can teach similar lessons to your kids from a young age. For example, your child may want a third Lego set, but do they really need it? When you teach your kids to differentiate between wants and needs, and to practice gratefulness, you are less likely to encounter the refrain of "Can I have this? Or that?"

As Venerable Dr. K. S. Dhammaratana noted, "A grateful heart turns what we have into enough." The healthy psychological attitude you engender in your kid of realizing they have enough acts as a cushion to buffer and reduce many psychological problems. No child is too young to cultivate this kind of attitude. No parent is too busy to teach, practice, and role-model this valuable life skill.

"All of you have to eat what is on your plates. ..."

Being grateful: Practices and exercises

In this section, I offer some tips and guidelines for teaching kids simple gratitude practices. Regardless of their ages, your family can collectively or individually practice these exercises. I would advise you to adjust and simplify the exercises to suit the age of your child. For younger kids, I recommended that you do the exercises with them. I also share some personal stories to demonstrate the powerful insights you and your child can gain from these experiences.

Gratitude meditation for the mind and body

On waking up each morning, encourage your child to take a few moments to quieten their mind and practice being grateful to the mind and body, saying, "I am alive and breathing. Thank you for looking after me during the night." This can be done while they are either lying down or sitting up in bed. Your child can thank each part of the body in turn – for

example, "Thank you, breath. Thank you, heart. Thank you, feet." This simple meditation can be practiced by kids of all ages, and for as long as they are able to sustain their attention. It is helpful for you and the whole family to take part in this gratitude meditation too. I practice this meditation each morning, silently thanking my mind and my body for enabling me to enjoy the beautiful morning.

We are usually aware of our minds and bodies when something does not feel quite right, and we are less aware of them when we are feeling fine. According to leading American mindfulness expert Jon Kabat-Zinn,[25] as long as we are breathing, there is more right with us than wrong with us, no matter what is wrong. As an example, I share a lighthearted but a valuable personal experience of discovering this kind of attitude.

"I am alive and breathing. Thank you for looking after me in the night."

"I can still pee"

Many years ago, while getting my garden ready for my daughter's summer wedding, I planted some beautiful annuals. One very hot day (about 40 degrees Celsius, or 104 degrees Fahrenheit), I rushed home from work to water the annuals. Even from my car, which I'd parked in the driveway, I could see the plants were already withering. I ran from my car and started watering, forgetting to leave the car's handbrake on. Suddenly, I saw my car rolling down the driveway, crashing through my front gate, and careering towards the house of my neighbor Tom across the road. My car – a red Holden Barina, which I affectionately named Serena – landed on top of Tom's letterbox.

I called roadside assistance to tow away my car. I can still recall my conversation with the roadside assistance man, Colin, when he arrived and saw the scene.

"I've never seen an accident like this before," Colin told me. "Are we on Candid Camera [the famous television show where people were unknowingly filmed for their reactions to unusual situations]?

"No," I replied. "This is real. I forgot to put on the handbrake."

"When are you planning to drive again?" he asked.

"I don't know. When the car is repaired. Why?"

"Because I don't want to be on the road when you are driving!"

Colin and I chuckled, as his observations were funny but spot on. Later, I got a lift to my office as I had a client waiting. Due to the extreme heat, the air-conditioning had broken down and the office was sweltering. I went to the restroom and sat on the toilet. I felt utterly overwhelmed.

Lynne's wedding is in a few days, I thought. The plants in the garden are withering. Serena is sitting on top of Tom's letterbox. The air-conditioning in my office is broken. What else can go wrong?

Suddenly I started to laugh. A friend washing her hands outside called out, "Are you okay?"

My little car Serena landed on top of Tom's letterbox.

"Yes. I'm okay," I laughed. "I can still pee."

And I was okay. Walking back to my office, I had the insight: When all else failed, my body did not. And I was grateful.

In my office, my client, a senior manager, shared her problems and explained how overwhelmed and stressed she was feeling at work. I listened to her quietly and recounted my disastrous events of the day.

"No matter what was wrong with my day," I concluded, "there is more right with me, because I can still pee."

"I am ok. I can still pee."

My client saw the lighter side of my experiences. We had a good laugh, and she finished her counseling session in a better frame of mind. A few days later, she emailed me about another stressful day at work. She ended her email with this:

> But I am okay. I remembered your hilarious circuit breaker and used it myself. I went to the restroom, laughed and said to myself, "I can still pee." I really felt better and grateful that my body is still doing well even though my day is not. You should really write a book titled "I can still pee." It worked.

I never wrote that book and I'm now sharing this anecdote in writing for the first time. Despite the personal nature of my experience, every time I share the story with other people, like my client, they laugh and tell me that the circuit breaker worked for them as well. Although lighthearted, the experience taught me the value of prioritizing what is really important – our health, which we often take for granted – rather than focusing on the negative things that have happened to us. So, now each morning I thank my mind and body for looking after me well, as I remember the timely cue: "I can still pee."

I recommend that you help your child try an analogous exercise when they go to the bathroom. Or even simple practices such as:

- "Feel your heart going thump-a-thump and say 'Hello!'"
- "Feel your little toe wriggling and say 'Hi!'"
- "Smell the cookies and feel how your mouth is watering."

This is a fun way to introduce an easy circuit breaker to help your kids to be mindful of their senses, feelings, sensations, and overall physical health, and to appreciate that their bodies are still working even when they are feeling down, stressed, or anxious. These supportive exercises, which are designed to help kids engage in gratitude meditation, can augment the practices I describe in Chapter 7 for cultivating a "beginner's mind."

Inter-relatedness and interconnectedness meditation

In Chapter 1, I discussed the ideas of inter-relatedness and interconnectedness and shared Thich Nhat Hanh's beautiful account of interconnectedness in nature, the renewal of the leaves, and the tree. Closer to home, you can help your kids appreciate inter-relatedness with some simple daily practices. For example, at breakfast, whatever the kids are eating – raisins, cereals, bread, or porridge – ask them to maintain a few moments of silence and to be mindful of how the breakfast item ended up on their plates. You can use any breakfast food for this exercise.

Eating raisin meditation

To illustrate this practice, I use the example of eating a raisin,[26] inspired by the eating raisin meditation popularized by Kabat-Zinn. You can use this meditation to encourage your child to practice gratefulness for all the elements that went into the production of the raisins. Invite your child to:

Eating raisin meditation.

- slow down their eating, pay attention to the texture, color, and quality of the raisin, and watch how the mind anticipates eating the raisin
- be mindful of all the elements that enrich and nurture the grapevines, such as the soil, sun, and rain
- thank the farmers who till the soil and harvest the grapes, the people who produce the raisins, and yourselves – the parents who serve the raisins for breakfast.

There are two important learnings for your kids from this kind of meditation. The first is that they learn to be mindful of every element that contribute to the raisins being on their plates. The second is the reflection that if any of these elements were missing, they would not be eating this particular breakfast. In this way, you show your kids how to appreciate and to be grateful for how things are interconnected and to thank everyone for making them whole, just like the raisins. David Steindl-Rast,[27] a renowned Benedictine monk and interfaith scholar, promotes the simple message that happiness is born from gratefulness. According to him, it is not happiness that makes us grateful, but rather gratefulness that makes us happy.

Grateful for everything and nothing meditation

As a psychologist, my day is often full helping clients with their problems and concerns. I am aware that at the end of the day, my mind is filled with thoughts about work. So, I have made it a practice as I walk to my car to slow down and do a walking meditation, focusing on my feet as I walk. In the car, I pause before starting the engine and watch my breath in order to quieten down my mind. I practice gratitude, noting that during the day everything had ended relatively well and nothing dramatic has happened. I call this exercise the "Grateful for everything and nothing meditation."

You can initiate a similar practice at home:

- When your kids come home from school, or you return from work, encourage each family member to take a few moments to pause and quieten down their minds, thereby reducing the internal dialogue about the day's goings-on.

- Practice being grateful that each of you have arrived home safely. If you are mindful that anything could have happened in 24 hours, then you can be thankful that everything is well, and nothing happened, and be grateful for an uneventful day.

To practice this simple exercise, I recommend that – as your kids are being picked up, as you park your car, as each of you take off your shoes, change your clothes, put down your bags, phones, computers – you learn to do these activities slowly and

"Everything is well, and nothing happened. We are thankful for an uneventful day."

mindfully, focusing on your breath as you all perform each task. This simple mindfulness practice of slowing down and being grateful settles the mind and body into a state of calmness after a hectic day. It provides an emotional sanctuary for the family to enjoy the rest of the evening.

Psychological Explanations and Key Learnings

During my work with families as a psychologist for more than 25 years, I have come to appreciate and strongly believe that feeling grateful, being grateful, and expressing gratitude are the most important life skills you can practice and role-model to your child. Gratefulness is built on being mindful. Gratitude enriches and infuses us with kindness, thankfulness, and appreciation. Helping your kids be grateful builds the necessary foundation for them to learn to be spiritual, positive, resilient, imaginative, and nimble.

In our early years, most of us were taught as kids – and in turn, teach our kids – to say "please" and "thank you" when gifted with something. These were early developmental lessons in expressions of gratitude and appreciation. As we grow up, the gifts we receive are often more subtle for example, receiving emotional support, encouragement, a hug, a phone call, timely advice, or counseling. These psychological "Ps and Qs" are even more important to encourage if we wish to avoid inculcating in our kids a sense of entitlement.

I believe that one of the greatest buffers against feelings of stress, isolation, negativity, depression, and anxiety – some of the major catalysts for today's major mental health problems – is to practice a healthy sense of gratefulness ourselves and encourage our kids to do the same. The exercises and practices I have recommended are aids for cultivating and maintaining a continuously thankful and grateful attitude throughout the day. They are exercises that you and your family can incorporate into your daily lives easily, as they do not require you to set aside special times. However, the exercises do require a commitment to practice as often as you can. If you bookend yours and your kids' day – starting the day by grounding your minds and bodies in gratefulness and ending it by wrapping yourselves in gratefulness – you and your family can experience transformative, positive changes to your relationships with the world and the people in your lives.

I do not know of anyone who has overindulged in too much gratitude, kindness, thankfulness, or appreciation, as these values generate a healthy state of mind and attitude. More importantly, the practice of these positive values is free and there are no negative side effects, even when you and your kids binge on the practices.

Practice Guide

- Keep the exercises and practices age-appropriate, fun, and interesting.

- Work with simple and home-based activities whenever possible.

- Work with your kids to adapt and refine the exercises.

- Encourage your kids to discover the deeper and profound insights themselves.

- Encourage your children to extend gratitude, thankfulness, and appreciation to people and things, big or small.

Let me conclude this sixth and final theme in the Spring kids' treasury with a simple poem I wrote.

Grateful

As a Spring kid, I am grateful to ...

My parents for their gift of life, love and kindness,

My mind and body for taking care of me,

Nature for teaching me about hope and renewal,

The sun for warming my face as I stand in the breeze,

The rain for caressing my face as I dance in its gentle spray.

As a Spring kid, I am grateful for ...

The way I am intimately connected with everything,

With my parents and my body,

With nature, the sun, and the rain.

In turn, I will care for my kids mindfully,

When I too become a parent.

"I am grateful to the rain for caressing my face
as I dance in its gentle spray."

Part 2

Buddha and Animal Friends
Talk to Kids

Meet:

The picture gallery.

Part 2 is a guide for parents to help kids learn how to apply the wisdom and practices of the Buddha's teachings. Chapters 7–10 feature inspiring tales adapted from the Buddha's life and teachings, and from Zen stories and koans. Zen stories and koans are short stories used in meditation to help individuals cultivate a deeper understanding of the nature of things.

When my grandsons Matthew and Nicholas were growing up, I was constantly searching for simple stories to help them make sense of their experiences and feelings when they encountered unique or challenging situations. The lack of relevant material in the marketplace made me turn to the stories from the Buddha's life and teachings, Zen stories, and koans. Each chapter introduces a vignette based on the original Buddhist story, such as the tale of the monk and the scorpion. For many years, I used these vignettes as practice exercises with my grandsons and encouraged them to create their own stories and apply the morals from the teachings to real-life problems faced by their peers.

Chapters 7-10 provide examples of how Matthew and Nicholas have understood and used the teachings and stories. In these chapters, I offer important psychological interpretations of the Buddhist tales, Zen stories, and my grandsons' explanations, with key learnings and a practice guide. I also provide simple exercises and instructions for you to adapt the stories and use them with your own kids.

In Part 2, you will learn how to:

- teach your children to meditate and to practice mindfulness

- help your kids integrate the exercises and benefits of meditation and mindfulness into their lives

- use the vignettes to help your child cultivate being a Spring and Great kid

- help your kids to apply the learnings from the vignettes to manage their concerns and psychological issues

- adapt the vignettes or use comparable stories about inspiring role models, or from other wisdom traditions, to use with your kids.

Chapter 7

CULTIVATING A BEGINNER'S MIND

With mindfulness and meditation

"When your mind is not full of things, you can see clearly and understand everything."

– Conrad, the teddy bear

I have been teaching professionals, families, parents, and kids mindfulness and meditation practices for many years. I am often asked: "Can kids learn such practices and skills?" "At what age can the kids start?" "How do we teach them?" "What can we teach them?" My answer to the first two questions is yes, children can be taught mindfulness and meditation from a young age. However, the "How" and "What" questions are more involved and require some careful considerations.

Mindfulness and meditation practices have been introduced in many schools worldwide for kids of all ages. They are useful skills for your children to learn. This chapter outlines instructions and exercises for you to teach your kids these practices and provides an extensive discussion on the benefits of these skills. It includes:

- what meditation is
- understanding a beginner's mind
- the main types of practices: concentration and mindfulness meditation
- meditation instructions
- putting meditation and mindfulness into practice through illustrations and examples
- a psychological perspective on the benefits of and insights from meditation and mindfulness practices
- a practice guide and tips.

What is meditation?

Generally, meditation involves a set of mental exercises that enables us to quieten down our minds, still our thoughts, and learn to focus. All these exercises help us relax and improve our general well-being. You may be familiar with the various types of relaxation techniques, including meditation, yoga, and muscle relaxation exercises. However, Buddhist meditation and relaxation are not one and the same.

Although meditation is commonly associated with Buddhist practices and ideas, meditation per se is not unique to Buddhism. Other religious traditions, including Christianity, Islam, and Hinduism, have their own meditation practices for centering the mind and body. However, in my view, the Buddhist approach that informs my book offers a systematic and rigorous way of understanding the workings of the mind and body.[28] In Buddhist classical texts, the word meditation is not used. The actual term used is bhavana, a Pali word meaning mental culture and development. This is because what is important in the Buddhist practice is not just training our attention and increasing our concentration and awareness, but also the cultivation of positive mental qualities, including a beginner's mind, acceptance, and letting go. I will elaborate on this further.

Understanding a beginner's mind

A beginner's mind known as shoshin in Zen Buddhism involves embracing a "not-knowing" attitude: seeing everything clearly, without making hasty assumptions or quick judgments about a situation. Kids have this beginner's mind. A child's world is full of wonder and excitement, and children approach it with curiosity and endless questions.

Anne Bancroft,[29] the author of many Buddhist books, offers a good description of a beginner's mind. According to Bancroft, our minds are usually full of thoughts and have a resident commentator that passes continuous judgment on what we perceive. She explains that meditation in Buddhism is a way of quietening the mind and discarding this internal narrator, so that we see the world as it is instead of judging it as good or bad.

Cultivating a beginner's mind is an important foundation in meditation and mindfulness practice, but it is not generally well understood by or taught to practitioners. Most meditation and mindfulness exercises are used for relaxation and reduction of stress. However, as I show in this chapter, teaching your kids to cultivate a beginner's mind during these practices is essential.

The main types of meditation practices

From a Buddhist perspective, two kinds of meditation are recommended, namely concentration and mindfulness meditation. There is a tendency to conflate these two practices. However, if you are using the Buddhist approach, it is important to understand their essential differences and what each meditation involves, so that you know how to use them for yourself and for your kids.

Concentration or tranquility meditation

Concentration meditation, also known as tranquility meditation, helps to quieten down the mind. It reduces the tendency for the mind to ruminate. By focusing on one object – usually the breath or other objects of attention – to the exclusion of other mental distractions, the mind settles down and the internal dialogue is reduced. The essence of this practice is that the mind cannot hold two incompatible thoughts at the same time; for example, you cannot feel full and hunger concurrently. Similarly, if you have negative thoughts and feelings, and you focus on something neutral (like the breath) or a positive thought, or even listen to some soothing music, these negative elements will dissipate naturally. This type of meditation is usually described as the formal practice of meditation.

Insight meditation or mindfulness practice

While the Buddha promoted concentration meditation as a way of settling the mind, he emphasized insight meditation, or what is popularly known as mindfulness practice. When you calm down your mind, you have the mental capacity to gain insight or awareness into the nature and workings of your mind. In insight meditation, you are encouraged to bring your awareness to whatever enters your mind, and to be mindful of what you observe – your thoughts, feelings, emotions – and just to give them the barest of attention, without rejecting, repressing, or identifying with them.

Take the example of thoughts. Without adding value to them or trailing after them, you will notice that your thoughts soon pass away. Through mindfulness, you arrive at the understanding that everything, including your thoughts, emotions, and feelings, naturally arise and fall away if you do not get attached to them. On the other hand, trailing after your thoughts causes more and more thoughts to arise.

Usually, your mind is full of thoughts, stories, and running commentaries; seeking new stimuli; thinking about the past or the future but not really aware of what is happening in the present. The idea of meditation and mindfulness is not to empty your mind, but to maintain a continuous awareness of the state of your mind, whether it is anxious, distracted, or calm. The practice is also not to change your thoughts, but to change your relationship to your thoughts, by letting them be. Mindfulness practice helps you observe nonjudgmentally whatever enters your mind, and return your mind again and again to the present moment. In this way, you train your mind to stay focused on what is actually happening to you and for you. I would describe this as good mental hygiene.

The Buddha taught not only mindfulness, but practicing right mindfulness. We are all mindful; if we were not, we would probably not survive. For example, you teach your kids to be mindful of oncoming cars when they cross the road, and you are mindful not to give out your personal information to unknown callers. However, right mindfulness in Buddhist practice is more than awareness. Practicing right mindfulness means training yourself to stay focused on cultivating skillful and positive states of mind, and setting aside unskillful or negative states. Understanding the distinction between mindfulness and right mindfulness is crucial, as the latter can bring about profound insights and changes for you and your kids. I will elaborate further on the importance of practicing right mindfulness when discussing the benefits of meditation.

We could describe a mind that is full of distractions as mind-full, and a mind that is free from distractions as mindful. It is important to know when you are mindful and when your mind is full. Although it is not necessary, it is quite common to combine the two practices, using concentration meditation as a scaffolding to settle the mind, and mindfulness practice to stay present and embody a positive attitude.

Meditation instructions

I encourage you and your child to learn to meditate together. Some of the benefits of doing so include your ability to self-regulate and manage your own emotions, role-model the importance of meditation to your child, and share mutual experiences. I have combined the instructions for both concentration and mindfulness practices. You can adapt these instructions and the length of the practice to suit the age of your child.

First, with the help of your child, select:

- a quiet location
- a comfortable position, whether sitting, lying down, or walking
- comfortable clothing
- an object of attention – this could be the breath, guided instruction or imagery, or a meditative activity.

Secondly, as you meditate together, guide your child with oral instructions, giving the instructions clearly. Remember to take the practice slowly and allow for pauses in between each instruction to let your child follow your instructions easily. Use the words "And relax" to help your child to ease softly into the practice. If you have a bell, you can ring it three times to signal the start and end of the exercise.

Ring the bell (3 times) to indicate the start of the practice.
You can say the following aloud to your child:

Be aware of your breath. Notice your breath coming in and out of your nose [encourage your child to focus on wherever your child notices the breath, on the chest or the stomach]. And relax.

Let your attention stay with your breath.

Breathe in deeply and breathe out slowly. And relax. There is no need to breathe in any special way. Just follow your normal breathing.

Notice any thoughts coming up in your mind.

Notice any feelings and sensations coming up in your body.

Let your thoughts, feelings, and sensations go. Bring your attention back to your breath. And relax.

You will soon notice your mind wandering. This is okay. This is what the mind does. Just gently guide your mind back to your breath.

If your mind wanders off a hundred times, try and bring it back a hundred times. And relax.

Ring the bell (3 times) to signal the end of the practice.

As mindfulness is a way of being aware of what you are doing or experiencing, there are different exercises you can use to help your child practice, such as eating mindfully, walking mindfully, or coloring mindfully. You could even encourage your kids to help you to make their beds, put away their toys, feed their pets, or water the garden mindfully. It is the attitude of being present, rather than the activity itself, that is important. In Chapter 6, I provided additional examples of how you and your child can incorporate mindfulness exercises into your family life easily.

Putting meditation and mindfulness into practice: Illustrations and examples

The most important insights of the meditation exercises come when the training is put into practice in real life. In this section I share the activities and exercises I used with my grandsons Matthew and Nicholas when they were aged between 2 and 7 years old. I hope the following accounts will help you to:

- learn how to adapt the exercises to use with your children
- understand your kids' level of understanding of the practices
- appreciate the insights that even young kids can gain from the practices
- understand the more profound benefits of meditation and mindfulness.

From a very young age, I taught Matthew and Nicholas how to meditate and cultivate mindfulness using the instructions I described above. I made sure these practices were carried out when they agreed to do them, and to keep the duration of the exercises short and sustainable. I meditate with them and invite them to discuss their experiences at the end of the session.

I also taught them to be aware and to be mindful of their thoughts, feelings, and emotions as these arise in their minds, and to let go of them through simple circuit breakers such as releasing their thoughts and feelings into balloons and soap bubbles, letting the thoughts float to the sky, or replacing negative thoughts with happy memories. You can use your own creativity to introduce fun and engaging circuit breakers to help your child learn to let go.

Another important lesson I helped Matthew and Nicholas to understand is how they feel when their minds are full of thoughts and distractions, and how they feel when they clear their minds. In this way, they have learned to experience the difference between being mindful and mind-full.

I also introduce my grandsons to the more subtle insights that ground meditation and mindfulness, and that are not often taught to kids. One of these most important insights is the cultivation of a beginner's mind.

Initially, children may not understand why they are meditating. To help your kids to understand the practice, you could involve them in writing stories based on their experiences. In this way, your kids will start to see the meaning and value of their training. From their stories, you will also start to appreciate the extent and depth of their understanding. This is what I encouraged my grandsons to do through storytelling and discussions. The following are two accounts from Mathew and Nicholas that helped me understand what they have learned.

Clearing and calming the mind: Matthew's made-up story

Children love writing stories. I have been collaborating with Matthew on storytelling since he was a young child. At age 2, Matthew composed a story which I recorded. The narrative showed his understanding of his meditation and mindfulness practices, and how he applied this understanding.

Matthew wrote about his lead character Toby and his teddy bear Conrad. (Conrad was gifted to him by the Conrad Hotel in Singapore where we stayed when he was a toddler. Matthew takes Conrad with him everywhere.) In the park, Toby encountered three imaginary friends. Matthew injected humor into the storyline by the answers the imaginary friends gave to Toby's questions. The following are some extracts from Matthew's story.

"The adventures of Toby: Nobody, somebody, everybody"

Toby said to the three kids, "I am Toby. What is your name?"
    The little boy answered, 'Nobody."
    Toby said, "You can't be nobody. You must be somebody."
    The second boy laughed and said, "That's me!"

Toby was puzzled. "Where is everybody?"

The little girl replied, "That's me."

Toby asked, "What is your name?" The girl said, "Everybody."

The three children laughed and ran off.

Toby was confused. At home he asked Conrad to help him to understand the children's behavior.

Conrad said, "Your mind is too full of ideas and thoughts. You are trying too hard to understand. You need to relax."

Conrad guided Toby in some meditation exercises.

"Close your eyes. Place your hands at the side of your body, as if you are sleeping. Try and breathe in very deeply. Like you trying to drink your breath."

Toby took in a deep breath.

Conrad continued, "Now let your breath out slowly, like you are blowing a bubble."

Toby let his out breath slowly. "This is fun. I am feeling better."

Conrad continued, "Open your eyes, and look up at the sky and clouds. Let your thoughts float away like the clouds."

Toby looked up at the sky and allowed his thoughts to float away – one thought at a time. He was surprised.

"When your mind is not full of things, you can see
more clearly, and understand everything."

"Look, Conrad, the clouds are moving. They keep changing their shapes and sizes. They don't stay the same. Like my thoughts. That is interesting.'

Toby kept breathing in and out. Slowly, his mind started to clear. After a few minutes, he said, "Conrad, I am not confused or anxious anymore. I understand that the children were teasing me when they told me their names. They were being funny. I like that."

Conrad explained, "When your mind is not full of things, you can see clearly and understand everything."

Cultivating a beginner's mind: Discussion with Nicholas

Since he was 3 years old, Nicholas has been learning meditation and mindfulness with me and his teacher at school. A note from his teacher described some of their practices.

The children reflected on the way their body felt as they practiced relaxation and meditation techniques. ... One experiential exercise involved the children meditating on the sky and the rainbow.

I was intrigued with what Nicholas had learned from his practices, and discussed his understanding in an interview with him that I conducted when he was 7 years old. We talked about his meditation experiences in school, and his insights. I have quoted fairly extensively from his reflections to show the insights and learnings that kids can gain from such simple practices. The following are extracts from our discussion.

On interconnectedness

"Nicholas," I said, "when you were in school, you asked your teacher, 'Does the rainbow remember that it was a raindrop before. What do you mean?'"

"I was asking, does the rainbow know it was a raindrop?" Nicholas replied. "I know the rainbow was a raindrop before."

"So you know it was a raindrop before. But you wanted to know whether the rainbow knew that?"

"Yes."

"Sounds like you're saying that things have a cause and then there's a result," I said. "For example, when it rains, the rain falls onto the ground and the rain turns into a rainbow. In meditation we call it interconnectedness. There is a start, a middle and an ending."

"I understand," he replied.

On mindfulness: One "L" and two "L"s

"How do you feel after you meditate?", I asked.

"Mindful with one L," Nicholas replied. "It's basically the opposite of mind-full with two Ls."

"What's the difference?" I asked.

"Mindful with one L, it's not mind empty. It's emptier."

"What does mind-full with two 'LL's mean?"

"Just thinking a lot of thoughts."

"What happens when you are thinking a lot of thoughts? Why is that not okay?"

"It's not necessarily bad."

"Then why don't people like it?

"Because if you wanted to sleep and you're thinking about sleeping," Nicholas replied, "it never actually helps. It just makes you angry that you're not sleeping, which makes you not sleep."

"Okay," I said.

"If you're trying to think of a really good idea," he continued, "being mind-full with two LLs would be great. If you're trying to invent something, mind-full with two LLs would be great."

"Can you explain that?"

"When you are thinking a lot of thoughts, new thoughts will keep coming into your mind. And eventually you'll think of something really good."

"And when is mindful with one L important?"

"When you're sleeping, one L is good. Because when you're sleeping, you won't want to be thinking a lot of things. When you're trying to sleep, it's just harder when you're thinking of EVERYTHING."

"That's a good distinction," I said. "Do you do that yourself when you are trying to sleep? Do you have mindfulness with one L or two LLs?'

"Two Ls," Nicholas replied, laughing.

"Because you have a lot of thoughts?"

"Yep, exactly," he laughed. "Especially at night when I'm trying to sleep."

On managing thoughts, letting be, and letting go

"What do you do when you have those two Ls?" I asked.

"I wait for one L to go away." Nicholas laughed heartily.

"That's a good idea. How do you do that?"

"Wait, I guess."

"Do you watch your breath?"

"You just wait."

"Does it go away?"

"Yeah, eventually. Eventually your body's just too tired. It just starts to shut down. That's probably one of the most effective strategies for going to sleep. Because it always works."

"Everything does change and is not permanent. Did you have to do something for the one L to go away or did it just move away?" I asked.

"You just WAIT. That's what you have to do. You have to WAIT," he replied.

"Do you know what the Buddha called that? Change, that everything doesn't stay the same. Everything will change and move, and you just have to let it be and let it go. And that's how you get to one L. Does that make sense?"

"Yes."

"And that's why you meditate and watch your breath. You're not adding on more and more thoughts. Then the one L will go away," I said.

"I understand," Nicholas replied.

Benefits of meditation and mindfulness

Practicing meditation and mindfulness offers many benefits to kids. The more obvious benefits include learning to be calmer and to self-regulate, manage their stress and anxiety, and improve their overall well-being and emotional health. The following are some of the more subtle benefits, from a psychological perspective.

Seeing things clearly

In Matthew's story, when the imaginary friends did not respond to Toby's overtures, Toby assumed they had rejected him, and so he judged them to be unfriendly. As a result, he became confused and anxious. When Toby learned to quieten his mind, with Conrad's help, he was able to see things more clearly. He saw the kids' behavior with a beginner's mind and was able to appreciate the humor in their actions. "Conrad," he said, "I understand that the children were teasing me when they told me their names. They were being funny."

Understanding change and transformation

The exercises that Conrad taught Toby are analogous to the meditation and mindfulness practices I used with Matthew and Nicholas from a young age.

After Conrad instructed Toby to watch the clouds and let his thoughts float up to the sky, Toby was able to appreciate the change and transformation both in nature and in his own thinking. "Look, Conrad," he said, "the clouds are moving. They keep changing their shapes and sizes. They don't stay the same. Like my thoughts. That is interesting."

Cultivating a beginner's mind and a deeper understanding of things

Earlier, I discussed the importance of cultivating a beginner's mind, which allows you to look at things from a fresh perspective. When you tap into your child's beginner's mind, you will learn much about kids' minds – their sense of wonder, the questions that they are curious about, and their views about the world.

A beginner's mind also helps kids take another person's perspective, as this attitude frees their minds from preconceptions and motivates them to try and understand things at a deeper level. In my discussion with Nicholas, he demonstrated this perspective-taking. He explained that he asked his meditation teacher whether the rainbow knew it was a raindrop, he knew that the rainbow came from the rain, but he wanted to know whether the rainbow knew. Nicholas wanting to know the more subtle question of whether the rainbow knew its source beautifully illustrates a beginner's mind – someone wishing to understand interconnectedness from the perspective of the rainbow.

Understanding the difference between mind-full and mindful

Another interesting theme in my discussion with Nicholas was his response to my question about how he felt after meditating. "Mindful with one L," he replied. Nicholas explained, using his own experience with sleep. His ability to explain the difference between mind-full and mindful clearly demonstrates the kinds of insights kids can get from mindfulness practice experientially.

Managing thoughts, waiting, and letting be

One of the important benefits of meditation and mindfulness practices is learning how to manage thoughts and thinking. Matthew and Nicholas showed two different ways of doing this. One way is by using concentration meditation, as Matthew did by focusing on his breath and letting his thoughts float up the clouds one thought at a time, until his mind settled down. The other way is by using mindfulness practice, as Nicholas did by just waiting and accepting that his thoughts would eventually move away.

Psychological Explanations and Key Learnings

I have discussed the benefits of meditation and mindfulness extensively, to show you the importance of really understanding the essence of these Buddhist practices. While much has been written about the more explicit benefits (important as they are) of these practices for kids, such as stress, anxiety reduction, and emotional regulation, there is less discussion and understanding about how much kids are able to get in touch with and embrace the more profound and intangible nature of their experiences.

I explained earlier that, from a Buddhist perspective, meditation and mindfulness (especially right mindfulness) are about cultivating and embodying positive values. You can see from my grandsons' accounts that they not only learned to calm down their minds, but they also learned about seeing things clearly, understanding change and transformation, interconnectedness, the difference between being mindful and having a mind that is full, and letting go. Their experiences show that children are never too young to learn such insights. It would be helpful for you to encourage your child to experience these spiritual dimensions too. I believe that children's meditation experiences can teach adults much about life if we adopt an open mind towards kids' insights.

According to Jon Kabat-Zinn,[30] a beginner's mind is equally wonderful for parents and kids to practice. Rather than seeing your children through the lens of your ideas and opinions about them, Kabat-Zinn advocates appreciating the wonder of them and seeing their amazing nature. I am grateful that in working with Matthew and Nicholas, I was able to see not only the amazing nature of young minds but also to experience myself the remarkable, beautiful world surrounding us with a beginner's mind.

Practice Guide for Mindfulness and Meditation Exercises

- Mindfulness and meditation are a practice and an attitude. Cultivate both.

- Kids have natural beginner's minds. Discover new possibilities with them.

- Explore and discuss with your kids their insights and learnings from the practices.

- Preferably, the parent/facilitator should have personal experience of and training in mindfulness and meditation practices. If not, consider working with a trained facilitator.

- Make the exercises relevant to your kids' current experience and interest. Encourage them to focus on an activity they are able to relate to, such as breathing, watching clouds, counting, and coloring. Think creatively about an object of focus you can use to help your child's mind settle down easily.

- Allow kids to vary the exercise as it unfolds. Ensure the exercise remains enjoyable, rather than another activity that they have to do.

- Keep the practices simple. Make the meditation exercise shorter than the level of concentration the child is capable of sustaining. This will help them gain mastery over their experiences, and give them a sense of competency.

- You and your children need to enjoy the exercise and be able to laugh at whatever f ows from the practices.

Chapter 8

RIGHT VIEW
AND RIGHT ACTION

The boy who did not stay burnt

**"When we really understand others, we might find
that we have many things in common."**

– Matthew

The story of Siddhartha, an Indian prince who left a life of luxury at his father's palace, gained enlightenment as the Buddha and brought his teachings to humanity, has inspired young and old for more than 2,600 years. Matthew was interested in learning more about the Buddha's youth and his teachings. In this chapter, I share how Matthew (then aged 11) used our discussion as an inspiration to write his own story about a boy who did not stay burnt.

The story: The Buddha's life and teachings

The Buddha was born as Prince Siddhartha Gautama in the kingdom of Lumbini. According to legend, it was prophesied that he would become either a great king or a great spiritual leader. Siddhartha's father sheltered him from all worldly suffering, hoping Siddhartha would succeed him as a king. At the age of 29, when Siddhartha stepped out of the palace for the first time, he encountered (separately) a homeless person, a sick man, and a person who had died. He also met a holy man who appeared to be quite content, despite being poor. Siddhartha was confused by what he saw. Several years later, in a quest to try and understand the suffering of human beings, he renounced his life as a prince and became a monastic person.

Siddhartha studied with many renowned teachers and religious leaders, and practiced various skills and techniques. However, none of his studies and training provided him with the answers he was looking for. After many years of wandering, as he rested under a large sacred fig tree (called the "Bodhi tree" or the "Tree of Awakening"), he gained the insight that he had to follow a "Middle Path" – that is, live a balanced life that does not swing towards the extremes of likes (attachment) or dislikes (aversion). Siddhartha became known as the Buddha ("The Awakened One") and taught for 45 years until he passed away at age 80.

The Middle Path, which is also called the Eightfold Path or the Fourth Noble Truth, is one of the Buddha's most important teachings. The Eightfold Path comprises the eight factors:[31]

1. Right view or understanding

2. Right thought

3. Right speech

4. Right action

5. Right livelihood

6. Right effort

7. Right concentration

8. Right mindfulness

I explained to Matthew that the word "right" is not about right or wrong, good or bad, but about being skillful. The term "skillful" means developing, for example, a clear or right understanding ("right view") of things and carrying out positive actions ("right actions"). Right view and right action help to free our minds from regret, fear, anger, and anxiety.

Matthew was inspired by the Buddha's life and teachings. He asked to write his own story based on Buddha's advice of "right view" and "right action." He imaginatively situated his story between two time zones: the present experiences of a group of kids in a school, and the past experiences of the Buddha during his growing-up years.

The following is a condensed version of Matthew's story.

The boy who did not stay burnt

Present day at school

Buddha was sitting near the local public school when he heard two boys shouting at a kid called Lin. Lin looked sad and dropped his head as he walked through the school gate, and the boys continued to laugh at him.

Buddha's past

He was playing inside the castle when a gang of boys walked past mocking him and shouting insults. The Buddha was surprised by their behavior, as he had done nothing wrong. They shoved him and told

The boys laughed at Lin's burnt face.

him he was a spoiled, rich kid and would never make a good ruler. He accepted the insults, knowing that they had no merit.

Present day at school

Buddha followed the kids to class and waited by the tree. At lunchtime, the boys ran out together. Lin sat by himself. Several people were laughing at his face, which carried burnt marks, scars, and wrinkles. The Buddha asked Lin how he got the scars. However, Lin took the question as a further attempt to harass him, and tried to walk away. The Buddha asked Lin again why people were laughing at his face. Lin replied that he was involved in a car accident when he was young, lost his family, and hurt his face. People had made fun of him ever since.

Present day at lunch

The other boys walked up to Lin and the Buddha while they were talking. The boys laughed, saying, "You got a friend for once, Lin." The Buddha stood up for Lin. "You should not act badly towards Lin just because he looks different. You should try and understand how he was burnt." However, the Buddha forgave the kids for their actions and asked if they had been hurt or bullied before. The boys said yes, but suspiciously. "Our parents were not kind to us at home." Buddha asked, "How does that make you feel?" The boys replied, "Not great." Buddha said, "That is what you are doing to Lin. He is also human and deserves better treatment."

The boys gained the insight that they have much in common – that they did not have many friends, were not well liked or well treated. Nevertheless, they could still help each other and be friends. The boys invited Lin to join them. Lin was happy to be accepted by the group. Like Buddha, he forgave them for their past actions as he realized

Cultivate true friendship based on right understanding and mutual respect.

that they did not understand the real reasons for his scars. For the first time, he did not worry about his scars. In his own mind, he did not stay or feel burnt.

Buddha was happy for them. He said, "I wished that I had friendships like that when I was a child." The kids disagreed. "You were a prince, and wealthy. So you didn't need friends." Buddha replied, "I was lonely, and no amount of wealth can make up for having friends. You boys are lucky to learn about acceptance and true friendship."

Matthew explained that the morals of the story are about empathy, right view, and positive behavior:

There is normally a reason people bully. It is may be because bullies do not have the right view or understanding and were not encouraged to do the right actions.

Money does not buy friendship.

When we really understand others, we might find that we have many things in common, even if we did not like them before.

Psychological Explanations and Key Learnings

It is heartening when the younger generation look to great spiritual teachers and inspiring leaders such as the Buddha, Jesus, Muhammad, Confucius, Gandhi, Mother Theresa, Nelson Mandela, and others as their role models. So, I was delighted when Matthew asked to learn more about the Buddha's growing-up years and chose the Buddha's teachings of right view and right action as a basis for his story.

Matthew showed that he understood the importance of right view when he wrote about how the Buddha asked Lin about his scars and encouraged the boys to do the same. When the boys gained insight into Lin's condition, they were able to empathize, and then practiced right action and compassion by inviting Lin to join the group. Matthew demonstrated the benefits of positive role-modeling when he wrote about how Lin embraced the Buddha's example of forgiving people who had earlier not had the right understanding.

The Buddha also showed the importance of understanding the cause and effect of negative behavior by inquiring into the cause of the boys' bullying behavior. When the boys replied that their parents had not been kind to them, and that they did not feel good, we get a sense of their own insights into the negative effects of their upbringings on their behavior. Finally, the Buddha also taught the boys that real friendship is not based on wealth and status, but on right understanding and respect.

Matthew summed up his story well when he said that the key morals of the story are about good understanding, empathy, and positive behavior. Recently, when I was writing up Matthew's story for the book, I asked whether he would like to revise his story in any way. "Nai-Nai (Chinese for grandmother)," Matthew replied, "I am okay with you using my story as it is, if it helps kids to understand a situation clearly, and to do the right thing."

Bullying is a common experience for many kids today, whether from friends or on social media. Such experiences have a significant negative impact on kids. The way that Matthew used the Buddha's teachings to address bullying demonstrates a mindful way that you can help your own kids to deal with bullying behavior, regardless of whether they are the offender or the recipient. If your child has been bullied, try the following:

- Help them develop a right understanding by asking open questions, such as, "Why do you think your friend(s) behaved that way?"

- Help them understand that perhaps the other children may have experienced similar past experiences, or are copying such behavior from others. If this is the case, encourage your child to feel empathy and compassion for the perpetrators.

- Help your child communicate how they feel about the bullying to teachers, friends, and family, so they feel listened to and understood.

Once your child has developed some insights, you can encourage them to learn to forgive and let go of the impact of the bullying by discussing how it is their responses, rather than their reactions, that will empower them.

If your child is the offender:

- Encourage your child to reflect on their behaviors and feelings; for example, "How would you feel if someone did that to you? How do you think the other person feels?"

- Encourage them to take responsibility for their mistakes and practice compassion; for example, "Would you like to apologize and befriend the other person?"

Reflections and Practice Guide

It is important for you to help children cope with bullying. It is equally crucial that you teach them not to bully. You can help your kids refrain from such behavior by:

- sharing with them simple stories about positive role models

- helping them to make up stories based on the lives and teachings of teachers from different spiritual traditions.

One of the key learnings in this chapter is the importance of positive role-modeling. So when you are helping your kids reflect on their actions, it is helpful for you to reflect on yours as well:

- Do you seek to understand the real reason and cause of your children's behavior?

- Do you try and cultivate the right understanding of your kids' behavior before you respond?

- Do you role-model right actions such as empathy and compassion?

- Do you encourage your kids to cultivate true friendship based on right view and mutual respect?

- Do you practice forgiveness and letting go yourself?

Practicing right view and right action is the responsibility of every member of society, young and old. Use inspiring stories and teachings to help your child to become a responsible member of society.

Chapter 9

BEING OUR NATURE

The monk, the scorpion, and the mosquito

"Don't think that something is bad before you know why the person, animal or insect is doing that."

– Nicholas

The monk and the scorpion is a well-known Zen Buddhist parable told over the centuries to emphasize the importance of cultivating a deep understanding of one's true nature. There are many versions of the story. In this chapter, I have summarized the main themes in the parable. I discussed the Zen story with my grandson Nicholas (then aged 8) and encouraged him to write his own interpretation and application of the meaning of the story. I provide some psychological explanations on the story and Nicholas's exercise, and a practice guide.

The story: The monk and the scorpion[32]

Two monks were walking in the jungle. The older monk saw a scorpion struggling in the water. Knowing that scorpions do not like water, he extended his hand to help it out. The scorpion stung him. The monk dropped his hand in pain and the scorpion fell back into the water. The monk repeated his efforts. However, each time, the scorpion stung him and fell back into the water. After several attempts, the monk managed to save the scorpion and put it safely on dry land.

"Why do you keep rescuing the scorpion, knowing that it will sting you?" asked the younger monk, who was looking on.

The older monk explained that he was a monk and that it was in his nature to help. On the other hand, the scorpion was an insect, and it was in its nature to sting in order to protect itself. The monk added that both he and the scorpion were doing what was in their nature, and so there was no need to get upset or angry.

Below is Nicholas's interpretation and application of the story, which he titled "Nick's thing."

Nick's thing on the Buddha's teachings

My friends and I were eating lunch on the grass. A mosquito bit one of my friends. He tried to squash the mosquito. I remembered the story of the monk and the scorpion. I thought to myself that the Buddha would probably have advised, "Why do you need to do that? It is in the nature of the mosquito to bite. It's just getting its lunch."

"The mosquito is biting us because it is hungry. Imagine you trying to get some food, then someone tried to squash you."

I said aloud to my friends, "The mosquito was biting us because it was hungry. Imagine you trying to get some food, then someone tried to squash you. Let's go somewhere else to eat."

My friends stopped squashing the mosquito. We moved away from the mosquito and ate our lunch peacefully.

Nicholas explained: "The moral of the story is compromise and don't think that something is bad before you know why the person, animal, or insect is doing that."

Psychological Explanations and Key Learnings

What are some of the key lessons from the story of the monk and the scorpion? How can you apply the lessons to your parent–child relationship?

The monk's act of kindness in rescuing the scorpion illustrates the practice of compassion. Many of us offer conditional love to others. If someone behaves well, we treat them well. If they misbehave, we probably get annoyed. However, compassion, like a parent's love, is unconditional. If your kids misbehave and hurt you, you will still love them and do your best, regardless of their behavior. The monk treated the scorpion with compassion because it was in his nature to be kind and to help, just it would be in your nature to do the same for your child.

The older monk understood that the scorpion stung him to protect itself, and that it is in the nature of scorpions to react out of fear and anxiety. Equally, it was in the nature of the monk to help. The basic nature of most people is one of non-harm and kindness, as taught by the Buddha. So it was in the case of the monk. This means that when the scorpion stung him, he felt pain but not mental suffering because his actions were motivated by compassion and understanding. The monk was letting his best nature stand out. This is a good illustration of right view and right action (see Chapter 8).

Similarly, even though you and your kids may see things differently, try not judge their actions as "good" or "bad" until you have a better understanding of why they are behaving in that fashion. Understanding your child's nature, and the real reasons for their actions, may help reduce not only your feelings of disappointment but also, more importantly, the emotional suffering you may experience as a result of their behavior.

The moral of the story is that our behaviors and thoughts should be guided not by the nature of others but by our own nature of understanding, compassion, and empathy.

Nicholas's explanation to his friends that it is in the nature of the mosquito to bite, as it is looking for food, and his suggestion that they act with compassion rather than destroy the insect, showed that he understood the wisdom imparted in the Zen story well.

So when engaging with your child, it is important to understand what your child's real nature is. Take the example of Carol, whom I wrote about in the Introduction. Carol's lack of concentration in school was misdiagnosed by her doctor and psychologist as ADHD, when in fact she was a gifted child who was easily bored with the easy school subjects. When her mother understood how Carol really was and responded to her appropriately, Carol's "ADHD" symptoms dissipated.

It is equally important that you understand your own nature as a parent.

**Practice compassion based on understanding
rather than judging others.**

If you are mindful that you are an anxious parent, and unduly protective of your child, you can lower your anxiety by learning to see whether there is a real cause for concern about your child.

Try to adopt the takeaways which the animal friends share from this Zen story – strive to understand your own and another's nature, differences in nature are not "good" or "bad," just different. Allow your best nature to stand out and practice compassion based on understanding rather than judging others.

Practice Guide

- Share the Zen story with your kids when they are receptive to learning about such stories. In the case of a younger child, you could read the story aloud.

- Listen patiently to your kids' explanations and understanding of the story. Ask open-ended questions such as, "Why did the monk help the scorpion?" "Why did the scorpion sting the monk?" You could also invite the children to draw their explanations if they are not able to articulate them.

- Share Nicholas's exercise with your children.

- Encourage them to see the parallels between Nicholas's story and the original story, such as, "Why the mosquito bite the children? Is it the same as the scorpion stinging the monk?" "Why did Nicholas asked his friends not to hurt the mosquito?"

- Discuss with your kids how they might apply the learnings to their own experiences or those of their friends and families; for example, "How can you help others who might need your help?"

Chapter 10

IN DREAMLAND

Honesty is the best policy

**"Other people can use your own lies against you.
Do not lie."**

– Matthew and Nicholas

Zen stories are short parables infused with meaningful themes to help us to uncover the wisdom in the story at various levels. These insights can be understood at a simple, ordinary level, or at a deeper, penetrative one. Zen stories may at times seem puzzling and nonsensical. However, if you delve further into the hidden meaning of each story, it can produce real insights. This was the case with the Zen story called "In Dreamland." I shared this story with Matthew and Nicholas, who wrote their own interpretations and explanations of the tale from the perspectives of an 11-year-old and an 8-year-old, respectively. As in Chapters 7–9, I offer psychological explanations for the Zen parable, my grandsons' interpretations, and a practice guide.

The story: In Dreamland[33]

The story revolves around a teacher who took a nap every afternoon. When his students asked why he did this, the teacher explained: "I go to Dreamland to meet the ancient sage, Confucius, a renowned Chinese philosopher, who also took naps." The teacher added that during his naps, Confucius would dream of other ancient masters and bring back their wisdom to share with his followers.

One hot day, the students took a nap. The teacher scolded them for doing so.

"We went to dreamland to meet the ancient masters like Confucius did," one of the students responded.

"What was the message from the ancient masters?" the teacher asked.

"We asked them if our teacher went there every afternoon," the students jokingly replied. "The ancient masters told us that they have never seen or met our teacher."

"I go to dreamland to meet Confucius."

Matthew's interpretation

In the afternoon, the teacher would look at his mobile phone while the children were doing their tests. One day, the children decided that after they finished the tests, they were going to look at their phones too. The teacher told them that they are not allowed to do so. The teacher added, "I am allowed to use my phone because I am doing important work."

While he was talking, one student looked over the teacher's shoulder. The teacher was watching Netflix. In the school, teachers and students were not permitted to use their phones in the classroom. Now, whenever the children got in trouble for using their phones in class, they said, "We are doing important work."

Matthew explained that the morals of the story were:

- If you lie to others, they will not be able to trust you.

- Other people can use your own lies against you.

- Treat others how you would like to be treated.

Nicholas's interpretation

In school, the teacher checked his phone frequently. The students asked the teacher why he was doing that. The teacher said, "I am checking with the headmaster what to teach." The teacher was in fact looking at his holiday photos.

The next day, everyone brought their phones. The teacher asked, "Why did you all bring your phones?" The students said. "Just checking what the headmaster asked you to teach us." The teachers looked at his students with a guilty smile.

Nicholas explained that the moral of the story was: Do not lie.

"I am doing important work."

Psychological Explanations and Key Learnings

This lighthearted Zen story, while simple and humorous, contains important lessons about honesty, integrity, role-modeling, and self-importance. As we can see from the use Matthew and Nicholas made of the story, these themes remain relevant today.

While Matthew and Nicholas wrote their stories separately, they came up with similar themes about teachers lying about their real intentions, and the students being able to discern the truth and making fun of the teachers' clumsy efforts to hide it. Although the students' attempts to imitate the teachers' behavior appear humorous, they nevertheless demonstrate an important theme: of kids losing respect for adults because of their lack of honesty and integrity.

The Zen story also highlight another important learning: the addiction to devices. Schools, governments, and parents are concerned about kids' "addiction" to their mobile phones and social media. Measures are now being proposed to limit kids' easy access to these things – which is why you need to role-model positive behaviors for your child. It is a source of great concern when I witness parents frequently checking their phones and the internet when spending time with their kids. You may have encountered examples of similar behavior at restaurants, family mealtimes, and other social occasions. I find it equally troubling when mobile devices are used by busy parents to "nanny" young children. So the account of a teacher inappropriately using his phone during class time is an important story of restraint to share with parents and kids.

The fact that Matthew and Nicholas chose to base their stories around the teachers' use of their phones, while telling the students they were not allowed to do so, highlights kids' concerns with there being one standard for adults and another standard for kids. Hence Matthew's and Nicholas's advice: "Do not lie" and "Treat others how you would like to be treated." The story "In Dreamland" of the teacher failing to set a good example for his students applies equally to parent–child relationships.

At the deeper level, the Dreamland story also points to a person displaying an inflated sense of self-importance. The teacher felt compelled to hide his tiredness behind the higher purpose of seeking wisdom. While the need for an occasional nap is not wrong in itself, lying about it under the guise of seeking enlightenment is. The lie resulted in the students challenging the teachers' false claims. It would have been better if the teacher had been humble and honest enough when caught napping to admit that he was tired and had dozed off.

You might have witnessed similar examples of self-importance or self-focusing from some people when visiting famous locations. I have heard visitors express an interest in learning more about the Opera House, only to see them taking selfies as evidence that they had visited it rather than actually learning about this iconic landmark.

Reflections and Practice Guide

How would you use the Dreamland story with your kids? I recommend that you tell them the story and discuss:

- what they have learned from the story by asking open-ended questions such as, "What do you think of the teacher's checking their phones in the class?"

- the moral of the story: for example, "If you were the teacher, what would you have told your students?" "If you were the student, what would you have said to the teacher?"

- the importance of telling the truth about their reasons for their actions and behaviors, rather than giving false explanations

- the importance of taking responsibility for their actions.

There are lots of stories you can use to help your children to appreciate the importance of the moral, "Honesty is the best policy." You could use the Dreamland story and do a similar exercise with your kids to the one I did with Matthew and Nicholas. Or you could choose another age-appropriate story. For example, share with your children Aesop's fable[34] of the boy who cried wolf, which tells the story of a boy who repeatedly lied to the villagers that a wolf is attacking his sheep. Initially the villagers rushed to help him, but when they found out the boy was not telling the truth, they stopped believing him. So, when the real wolf attacked, no one came to help the boy, and he lost all his sheep. Invite your child to write their own story and explanation of the fable. Discuss with your kids the moral of Aesop's fable. Ask them open-ended questions like: "What do you think of the boy's behavior?" "How should the boy apologize to the villagers?"

More importantly, role-model the key learnings from the Dreamland story to your kids. To do so, I encourage you to reflect on the following questions:

- Are you honest about your own actions and intentions?

- Are you open about the real reason for your behavior?

- Do you hide your actions behind exaggerated explanations to impress others?

- If the real reason for your behavior is uncovered, do you apologize?

If you practice similar principles yourself, your kids will be motivated to emulate what you do, and learn the important lesson that there is not one standard for parents and another one for children.

Part 3

Tales from Therapy:
Empowering Kids

Meet:

The picture gallery.

In Part 3, Chapters 11–16 draw upon my counseling work with my young clients. The chapters demonstrate the person-centered approach and creative solutions I use with my clients featured in the picture gallery. In Chapter 17, I showcase a fictional counseling session with wood snake to demonstrate working with kids who experienced similar issues.

In each chapter I discuss:

- the contents – the issues and concerns of the kids and wood snake I counsel
- the process – the interpersonal relationship between myself and my clients, and the dynamic approach I take in helping them move from a sense of emotional vulnerability to a state of empowerment, cultivating personal growth and emotional well-being
- the psychological explanations on the approaches I take
- the key learnings from the counseling process

and provide a practice guide.

In Part 3, therapists, educators, and healthcare professionals will learn a range of therapeutic approaches, skills, and exercises to help their clients explore and manage their psychological and mental health issues. Parents will learn how to adapt and apply these skills, techniques, and exercises to use with their kids in everyday, nonclinical settings.

Chapter 11

KIDS ARE SMARTER THAN ADULTS

How kids manage family conflicts

"What kind of a doctor are you? My papa is sick. Can you help him?"

– Wen

It was 3.30 pm. Sheng, a 50-year-old single parent, walked into my office, leading a somewhat reluctant 8-year-old Wen. They sat down; Wen was tired after a long day at school. Sheng sat in the chair across from me, while Wen flopped into the chair farthest away from my desk.

Sheng, a highly qualified professional, was going through an acrimonious divorce with his wife and feeling overwhelmed by the custody proceedings in court. Wen demonstrated many of the emotional and physical symptoms of a child caught between two "warring" parents: rebelling, acting out at school, constantly fighting with his peers, not eating, and sleeping a lot. The school counselor had diagnosed him as anxious and depressed, and advised his parents to take him to see a psychologist to help him to deal with his emotional problems.

I had been counseling Sheng to help him to psychologically manage his medical problems, including advanced cancer. His mental health was also negatively impacted by his ongoing marital issues and his concerns for Wen. Sheng asked for my help in making a preliminary assessment of whether Wen needed to see his own psychologist.

Kids and family conflict

Sheng introduced me to Wen. "Belinda is a doctor."

"What kind of a doctor are you?" Wen asked. "My papa is sick. Can you help him?"

"I am not a medical doctor, Wen," I replied. "I am a psychologist, a doctor who helps people to talk about and understand how they are feeling."

Wen nodded. "Can I talk about what is bothering me?"

I smiled and invited him to do so.

Wen looked tearful. "I know that Papa is sick. Every time he comes back from seeing the doctors, or when he is fighting with Mama, he looks really sad. He doesn't eat and he sleeps a lot. I am worried about him. Can you help him? I try to help him, but I am only 8 years old."

"Please, tell me more," I said.

How kids strategize to manage family conflicts

Wen explained some of his efforts to reduce the conflict between his parents.

"Papa, when you give me the letters for Mama and presents, I take them back with me. But I hide them."

Sheng looked surprised. "Why?" he asked.

"In the letters you crossed out Mama's married surname, which is the same as mine," Wen explained. "You changed it to her maiden surname. If Mama saw that, she would get very angry with you. So, I hide the letters in the car, and I don't show them to her."

**"Papa, when you give me letters for mama, food, and presents.
I take them back with me. But I hide them."**

"If I take the presents home," Wen continued, "Mama will ask me about them, how much they cost, and why don't I play with the toys she gave me. And then she would talk about you not loving me as much as her. I get very upset. I get a stomachache. I get very tired. I ask to go to bed. I can't finish my homework. And my teachers get upset with me in school."

"Is that why your teachers gave you a bad report?" Sheng asked. "And why you had to stay back in detention for not finishing your homework?"

"Yes, Papa," Wen said. "But I can't tell them the real reason. It's okay if they get angry with me, rather than get angry with you and Mama."

Sheng looked stunned and was lost for words. He had obviously not known the real reasons for his son's recent behavior. Wen looked worried about sharing so much. They both looked at me.

I was touched beyond words. Wen's plans to help his parents were generous and compassionate.

"Wen, you are an amazing kid," I said softly. You understand Mama and Papa very well. You are worried about them fighting over each other's actions. And your solutions to help them not to argue are very thoughtful. You prefer your teachers to get upset with you rather than with your parents. You are very kind. They should be so proud of you. I am."

Wen kept silent but smiled at my words of support. I turned to Sheng. Tears were rolling down his face.

"Wen, I am so sorry that Mama and I have caused you so much pain and heartache by our thoughtless actions," Sheng said quietly between his tears. Thank you for showing us

Belinda: "Wen, you are an amazing kid. You prefer your teachers
to get upset with you rather than your parents."
Sheng: "Today I learned how wonderful and thoughtful my son is."

how to be kind and generous to each other. I will explain to your teachers why you didn't finish your homework, and why you were so sad at school. I will talk to Mama about our behaviors and try not worry you so much. Today, I learned about how wonderful and thoughtful my son is."

Wen cried and ran over to hug Sheng, "It is okay, Papa. I want you to get better." He turned to me.

"Thank you for helping me and Papa today," Wen said in a stronger voice. "I will finish my homework, and not hide things from Papa and Mama anymore. I feel better now."

They walked out of my consultation room holding hands, and Wen skipped all the way to the door. Wen did feel better. His parents still went through the divorce, but they did not fight over him or try to compete for his affections. They also agreed to joint custody.

Psychological Explanations and Key Learnings

As therapists, we often bear witness to significant pain and suffering. And the pain and suffering are enormous when a child is involved in situations such as divorce and custody proceedings. By providing Wen with a sense of safety to talk about his feelings, I was able to facilitate Sheng to look at Wen's actions and behaviors through Wen's eyes, rather than from just the perspectives of Wen's parents and teachers.

As Wen's real motivation for his actions unfolded, all of us could see how much thought he had put into his strategies to help his parents to reduce conflict, and to ensure his teachers maintained a good impression of them. If Wen had not been encouraged to share his concerns, he would probably still be diagnosed as a troubled, defiant child impacted badly by his parents' divorce. Wen was clearly affected by the marital situation. However, uncovering the rationale and motivations for his actions enabled his father to see him as he was: a thoughtful, sensitive child trying in his own ways to cope with a painful situation.

The Buddha advises: "Talk with the kids." Often, adults talk at the kids. Talking with kids means practicing quiet listening and keeping an open, beginner's mind (see Chapter 7). From a therapist's perspective, this stance involves focusing less on the manifest symptoms, as in the case of Wen, and remaining nonjudgmental about the underlying rationale for their actions.

I believe that all human beings have an intuitive sense of empathy and compassion, and I have found this to be especially true in working with children. When therapists learn to talk with, rather than at, and listen mindfully to kids, free from concrete thinking and preconceptions and without relying primarily on observable symptoms (important as they are), the sense of empathy and compassion that flows from the therapist to the client can be transformative – regardless of the age of the client. The therapist connects with the humanity of the client, and the client connects with their authenticity and sense of empowerment.

It concerned me deeply to think what might have happened to Wen had he continued to be perceived as "the presenting patient" (that is, the client with the problems), rather than a compassionate young person trying his best to help his family. It is noteworthy that Wen's actions were not a case of role reversal. He wasn't trying to re-parent his parents; in fact, they were not even aware of the underlying reasons for his actions. It was clear that Wen's actions were motivated by his sense of empathy for his parents' pain and suffering. Following the Buddha's teachings of nonjudgment and keeping an open mind, Sheng and I were able to see what a beautiful person Wen was. And I am certain that Sheng and his ex-wife have become better parents through their appreciation of their son's generous spirit.

The problems that Wen experienced are not unique to a clinical or a divorce situation. Many kids encounter similar emotional issues when there is discord in the family. You can generalize and use the processes and techniques I employed with Wen in communicating with your child across many situations. Seek to understand your kid's concerns by first giving them an emotional safe space to open up about their thoughts and feelings. Try to use open-ended questions: for example, "Tell me more," or "Can you elaborate further?" Listen mindfully to your child's underlying motivations, and focus on their emotions rather than on their behavior. Reassure them that you empathize with any concerns they may have in sharing their feelings with you. And finally, acknowledge the amazing child you have brought up, as Sheng did.

You can use the following practice guide regardless of whether you are a parent or a clinician.

Practice Guide

- Provide kids with a sense of safety to talk openly and freely about their concerns and feelings.

- Listen mindfully to kids' explanations for their behavior.

- Avoid making early diagnoses. Explore the causes rather than just the symptoms.

- Avoid making hasty assumptions and reaching quick conclusions.

- Apologize for any misinterpretation of your children's behavior and acknowledge your own positive learnings from your kids.

Chapter 12

BE WHERE THE KID IS

Using circuit breakers and magic words

"You are trying to help me to understand why I get angry with Mummy and Daddy so much. ... I like that."

– Georgia

Maria brought her younger daughter Georgia, aged 7, to her first counseling session with me. In this chapter and Chapters 13–14, I share the therapy process and insights from my sessions with Georgia.

Georgia sat down reluctantly, looking annoyed. "I am angry with Mummy for asking me to come."

Maria, looking somewhat embarrassed, explained Georgia's reticence about seeing another psychologist.

"She is highly anxious and throws tantrums often. She gets angry with me and the family easily and often. My husband and I are finding it very difficult to cope with her. I took her to see a child psychologist before. Georgia couldn't relate to her, and we stopped after a few sessions. I felt that the psychologist was too theoretical and intellectual. We didn't find the sessions helpful."

"Georgia, do you know why you are coming to see me today?" I asked.

"Yes," Georgia replied, "I get upset and angry with Mummy, Daddy and Lucy [her older sister] a lot. I didn't like the other psychologist. She kept asking me to fill in forms. I didn't understand what she was trying to tell me.

"I also don't like it when Mummy gets stressed or Daddy yells," she continued. I would like them not to do that. I get upset when they get angry."

It was quite clear that Georgia's reactions were responses to her parents' outbursts, her sense of helplessness, and her desire to make things better. I suggested the use of circuit breakers using magic words. Georgia agreed.

Using magic words

"Would you like to help me prepare a list of magic words?" I said to Georgia. "You can use the magic words to help you relax or help your family to calm down when they are stressed or worried. Your list can include some praise for when they are doing okay. You can also prepare some magic words and praises for yourself as well."

"Georgia, would you like to help me prepare a list of magic words?"

Georgia pumped her fist in the air excitedly. "Yeah. I'd like to do that."

I explained to Maria that the list of magic words is a child's version of circuit breakers and mindfulness practice. I stressed the importance of use simple terms such as "magic words" to appeal to the child's sense of curiosity and imagination. More importantly, the list had to be designed by Georgia herself.

Family Member	Magic Words			Compliments
Mummy	*pineapple*	*salad*	*watermelon*	Good
Daddy	*grapes*	*orange 3*		Good job
Lucy	*coconut 2*			Good
Rover (the dog)	*good boy*			A treat
Georgia	*clam abdocer (word made up by Georgia)*			Good job

Georgia's list of circuit breakers.

It is interesting that Georgia chose words mainly from the fruit and food group and made up the word "clam abodcer" for herself. When a young client like Georgia designs their own list, it is essential that their choices are taken seriously. They also should not be asked why they have chosen certain words, so that it does not become an intellectual task.

Role-playing and discussion

To reinforce the use of the circuit breakers, Maria and Georgia agreed to my suggestion to role-play. Maria acted stressed and pretended to get angry. Georgia observed her behavior quietly and responded by using the magic words.

"Mummy, pineapple [pause] salad [pause] watermelon."

"Okay," Maria replied.

"Georgia, what would you like to say to Mummy now?" I asked.

"Good," she replied.

They both laughed. Georgia appeared to enjoy the role-play.

"Georgia, how do you feel?" I asked.

"Good."

"Maria, what do you think?" I asked

"Nice plan," Maria replied.

"Okay," Georgia said. I understand. I will try my exercise at home."

"Thank you," I replied. "I trust that you can do it."

"I will."

"I'm wondering how I would know that you will do your exercise," I said.

"Because you trust me," she replied. "I will do it because you trust me."

"Why do you think that I trust you?

"Because I trust you too." Georgia smiled.

Georgia and I shook hands and did a high-five together. To strengthen her understanding of the counseling session, I asked Georgia to tell me in her own words what she had learned.

"You are trying to help me to understand why I get angry with Mummy and Daddy so much," she said. "It is when they get stressed or yell at me, or when I'm afraid or lonely. You taught me to help them to stop so that I won't feel angry. I like that. I can learn not to be angry or stressed."

I was amazed at her insights and her ability to summarize her learnings from the counseling. At the end of the session, I asked: "Georgia, would you like to come back and talk to me again?"

"Yes, please," Georgia replied. "That was fun."

Psychological Explanations and Key Learnings

Georgia's wish to help others, especially her parents, was evident. It was important to motivate her by allowing her to express this. Empowering kids and working to their strengths before dealing with their symptoms and negative emotions is an important approach when working with kids, but it is not employed often enough in therapy. The conventional therapeutic approach is to delve into children's symptoms in the service of making a diagnosis. As important as diagnoses and symptom reductions are, I felt it was crucial to give Georgia a positive springboard to use in the future. Hence, I started the counseling with Georgia where she is – that is, from her own perspective and her expressed wish to reduce her concerns with her parents' behavior and to help them.

Although Georgia was only 7 years old, I found her to be highly intelligent, creative, and open to sharing and dealing with her issues. However, I realized from our discussions about her previous counseling experiences that Georgia needed an experiential rather than a theoretical approach, and that the traditional top-down approach of therapist and client would not sit well with her. I was also mindful that Georgia needed to be an active participant in the counseling process in a meaningful and engaging way. It was also important to establish a strong bond by ensuring we established a relationship based on trust. So I was delighted to hear Georgia say she trusted me because I trusted her – in other words, that the trust was reciprocal. An astute observation from a 7-year-old!

The practice of using magic words as circuit breakers is part of the therapeutic technique of behavior modification and emotional regulation using mindfulness. Given Georgia's age and previous counseling experiences, the behavior modification task needed to be simple, interesting, and punctuated with humor. It also needed to be set at a level that Georgia could appreciate and actively participate in; for example, by allowing her to design her own list.

Circuit breakers are analogous to using a meditative pause. For older kids, I usually recommend that they to count to 10 or observe their breath for a few minutes, in order to interrupt their rumination or negative thinking (see Chapter 7). However, it is more difficult for younger clients to embrace this practice, so I suggested a simpler exercise with Georgia: the use of magic words.

These provided the space for her to be mindful; to observe, pause, and interrupt her negative emotions, as shown in the role-playing. For circuit-breaking, you can use any simple activity that allows your child to pause.

Role-playing served a number of important purposes:

- encouraged Georgia to be mindful of her own and others' behavior

- reduced her reactions and allowed her to respond in real time, thereby reinforcing her own sense of agency and empowerment

- reinforced the key takeaways from the counseling session

- invited Georga to show appreciation when others behaved well

- helped her be aware of her own negative behavior and choose to behave positively.

Practice Guide

Whether you are a clinician or a parent, I recommend the following practices:

- Build a trusting relationship and encourage your kids to share their feelings freely.

- Depending on the age of the children, try to use simple, interesting exercises as a circuit breaker to promote behavior modifications. Get your kids' agreement to the type of circuit breaker to be used. Some useful examples are watching the breath, drawing, coloring, playing musical instruments, watering the plants, or playing with pets.

- Encourage the kids to participate and give them a lot of flexibility in designing the exercise.

- Role-play to ascertain your children's understanding and learnings from the exercise.

- Involve yourself (during therapy) or other family members (at home) in the exercise and role-play.

- Invite your kids to share their insights from the task and suggest ideas for improving the circuit breaker.

Chapter 13

TEACHING KIDS TO GIVE AND SHARE

Star ratings

**"I got more than five stars and lost one star.
I will try for eight stars next time."**

– Georgia

Georgia attended her second counseling session with Maria a few weeks later. In her first session, which I discussed in Chapter 12, I had provided Georgia with some skills and tools to help herself and others. The exercise, a child's version of mindfulness practice and behavior modification, involved the use of circuit breakers and magic words. Maria said that Georgia was enjoying the exercise and that she was using the magic words well.

"However, Georgia still gets angry occasionally," Maria added,

"Georgia, would you like to explain what Mummy said? I asked her.

"I like helping Mummy and Daddy not to get angry," Georgia replied. "I like helping myself not to get angry. But sometimes I don't do so well, and I still get angry."

Maria and Georgia laughed at Georgia's honest explanation.

It would appear that, despite the occasional lapses, giving Georgia the skills to regulate her own and others' emotions had reinforced her self-confidence. The approach had also deepened her own awareness of her reactions. We agreed to further focus on her strengths by encouraging her to take on more responsibility, learn leadership skills, and practice kindness, giving, and sharing.

I suggested another mindful exercise, which I called a "star rating plan," to add to the behavior modification plan detailed in Chapter 12. As with all the exercises, this task needed to be fun, experiential, pitched at Georgia's level, and involve her active participation.

The star rating plan

Maria, Georgia, and I discussed the plan. Georgia was given the liberty to decide on the number of stars she would be awarded for not getting angry with each family member, the stars she would lose if she got angry, and the stars that she would donate.

"Georgia," I said, "these are the star ruling rules we agreed on."

Star rating rules

Mummy

You are allowed to be angry with Mummy once a day.* If you don't get angry with Mummy each day, you will get one star.

When you get seven stars, Mummy and you can buy a present that you like.

---

*The rationale for allowing Georgia to react to Maria occasionally is to let her experience her default reactions in real time, and for her to make the decision about responding differently. I did not share this rationale with Maria and Georgia as I wanted Georgia to make this decision herself.

If you get angry with Mummy more than once a day, you will take away one star from the total. So, you can get a total of seven stars by not getting angry with Mummy.

You will get a bonus star if you do not get angry with Mummy for seven days – a total of eight stars.

Daddy

You will get three stars a week for not getting angry with Daddy.

Lucy

You will get three stars a week for not getting angry with Lucy.

Rover (dog)

You will get five stars a week for not getting angry with Rover.

"So, Georgia," I said, "you can earn a total of 19 stars if you do not get angry with the family and Rover for one week."

"What if I don't get angry with Mummy at all every day?", Georgia asked.

"That's good," I said. "Then you will get one star each day until you get 7 stars plus a bonus star."

"What if she has no star to begin with, and then she gets angry?" Maria asked.

"Then Georgia will owe Mummy some stars," I replied, "and she can deduct it when she gets some stars."

Kindness stars

I also discussed with Georgia the idea of including "kindness stars" in the plan – that is, stars she could give away from the total she earned – and how many stars she would like to give.

"Okay," Georgia said. "I understand. I'm excited to try it. I'll do my exercise."

Designing and using the star rating chart

Maria and Georgia came back for counseling again a few weeks later.

"She did the exercise immediately after our last session," Maria told me.

Georgia showed me the star rating chart she had designed and completed.

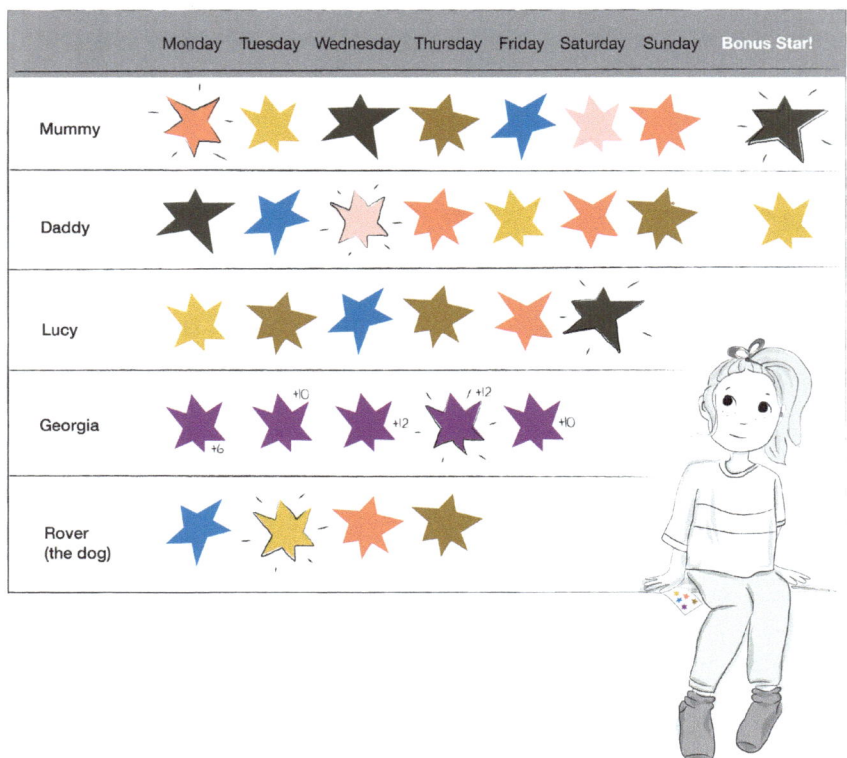

Georgia's star rating and kindness chart.

"The purple stars represent the times I was trying to communicate with Mummy, instead of getting angry," she explained. "+10 means I tried to communicate with her more than 10 times. Sometimes, I tried 12 times. Overall, I got more than five stars and lost one star. I'll try for eight stars next time."

"Well done," I said. "How do you feel?"

"Good. Sometimes I get a bit stressed because it is on top of my schoolwork. I get grumpy because I'm tired. And then I get angry. Mummy tries to calm me down. She drives me around in her car. It relaxes me. Or I squeeze Rover because he is like a teddy bear, and he kisses me back.

"I also learned to give and share my stars. I gave six stars to my sister Lucy, one star to Rover, one star to Mummy, and one star to Daddy. I kept seven stars for myself. I would like to buy a cot for my doll."

"You are very kind," I told her.

"Thank you," Georgia replied. "I like being kind and giving and sharing my stars with others."

Psychological Explanations and Key Learnings

In Chapter 12, we saw that Georgia was able to use the circuit breakers effectively to modify her behavior when she was trusted to take the lead. The exercise in this chapter continued to strengthen her awareness of her reactions, the reinforcement of her leadership skills, and her learning to embrace kindness and generosity. Georgia showed considerable leadership by designing her own star rating and kindness chart, and deciding how to use the chart to earn her stars and what to donate. It was a genuine display of autonomy and generosity.

It is important that when therapists begin working with a young child, the focus should be on helping the client learn alternative ways of behaving and responding to the world. It would have been easier, given Georgia's outbursts, acting out, and high anxiety, for her to be diagnosed as having "generalized anxiety" issues. And that diagnosis might have materialized had the primary focus been on her symptoms rather than on understanding the contexts and the familial dynamics in which these symptoms manifested. It is also crucial for therapists to give kids opportunities to learn more positive ways of behaving.

From my counseling with Georgia, it appeared that she had been caught in a pattern of habitual negative reactions and had difficulties with observing boundaries. The exercise of allowing her to decide on the star ratings, and to experience the joy of giving and sharing, afforded Georgia another way of mindfully interacting with her family and maintaining healthy psychological and emotional limits. When she experienced these positive feelings, her habitual patterns and symptoms appeared to dissipate.

Whether you are a therapist or a parent, I encourage you to use your own imagination to introduce fun ways for kids to learn to give and share. Some examples might include kids sharing their Christmas and birthday presents with the neighbor's children and friends, picking flowers from the garden to give to family members, or helping their parents clear the dishes after each meal. The list is endless. I also recommend the following guidelines when engaging with kids.

Practice Guide

- Try to understand kids' default responses and the triggers for their responses by asking open-ended questions.

- Use simple, interesting exercises to allow kids to experience more positive ways of behaving.

- Reinforce your children's sense of agency and competency by encouraging them to design their own tasks.

- Participate in the task during the counseling session, whether as a therapist or as a family member at home. Children learn much from seeing how other participants use the exercises.

- Discuss with kids their experiences, insights and learnings from the practices.

Chapter 14

EMPOWERING KIDS THROUGH ROLE-MODELING

The teacup of gratitude

"Why are you giving me the cup with both hands?"

– Georgia

Georgia, whose counseling sessions I discussed in Chapters 12 and 13, was making good progress. From the exercises we initiated and which she diligently executed, Georgia seemed to be happier, more settled, and less reactive. So, when Maria brought her to see me for her subsequent counseling appointment, we agreed that this would be Georgia's final session. After that, she would see me only if the need arose.

Role-modeling respect, appreciation and gratitude

During our final session, Georgia asked for a drink. I gave her some water in a Chinese teacup with both hands and showed her how to receive it and drink from it with both hands. I also gifted the cup to her as a present.

Belinda gifting a teacup to Georgia.

Georgia looked on attentively. "Why are you giving me the cup with both hands?," she asked.

I was impressed with her keen observation.

"When you give someone a present with two hands," I explained, "it is a gesture of respect. When you receive the gift and drink from the cup with both hands, it shows that you appreciate the present, and you are saying thank you to the giver."

Georgia put out both hands to receive the cup and drank from it.

"That is nice. I like that. Thank you."

I turned to Georgia and said quietly: "Mummy said that you are doing very well. And you are doing so well at home and school that Mummy and I thought maybe you don't need to come and see me for counseling anymore unless you want to."

Georgia nodded.

"Yes, Mummy and Daddy told me that. Is it okay if I come and see you again if I want to in the future?"

"Certainly, Georgia," I said. "I love working with you. And I am so proud of you. Would you like to share what you have learned?"

Georgia grinned.

"I learned that I could deal with my problems. That I am going to learn more each day. I learned about gratitude and kindness. I also learned ways to help at home. I learned to appreciate things and say thank you. Thank you, Belinda."

We gave each other a high-five. Georgia ran to Maria and gave her a hug.

Parents' acknowledgement of kids' personal growth

A few weeks later, Maria came to see me for her own personal counseling. Among other things, we discussed the joint sessions with Georgia.

Maria smiled, looking relaxed.

"Your exercises with Georgia were brilliant," she said. "She loves the Chinese teacup. When she gets upset at home, she takes out the teacup, pours some water in it, and drinks it with both hands. It calms her down. She offers the family drinks from the teacup with both hands too when she sees us getting stressed.

"Georgia loved her sessions with you. She said that the exercises were fun. You trusted her and gave her a lot of independence and autonomy. She is more confident now. I have seen a lot of progress in her behavior. She is not angry or anxious and when she is, she tries to explain her feelings. She hasn't used bad or angry words since her sessions with you. She even apologized a few times when she behaved rudely. She has never done that before."

"I am delighted to hear that, Maria," I said. "Georgia is very intelligent and sensitive. She learns very fast. And because I trust her, she trusted me. Mutual trust in a parent–child relationship is very important. She had a lot of anxiety previously because she picked up the negative vibes from you and James [Georgia's dad]. She is anxious about her parents fighting over so many issues. Her comment that she can deal with her problems is very insightful and has reinforced her self-confidence and resilience."

"I agree," Maria said. "There is a big difference in her when I manage my moods better. James is not so stressed too. Georgia does notice my stress, and reacts. We are in a better rhythm now. I try to praise her when she thinks of others. I acknowledge her capacity for empathy and kindness. Her relationship with James has much improved. He is home more often and picks the girls up from school.

"As for myself, I try to keep things lighter. I don't think that Georgia has a diagnosable condition. I learn to put things in perspective. She is doing well in school and has lots of friends. I shouldn't be so rigid and judgmental."

"Very nice insights, Maria," I said, "Good examples of mindful parenting and role-modeling. You should be proud of your own progress too."

Psychological Explanations and Key Learnings

The insight and acceptance from Maria that Georgia does not have "a diagnosable condition" is a powerful and meaningful statement. In my view, Georgia was not experiencing significant psychological mental health issues. Rather, her condition demonstrates that her problems were systematic, meaning that they took place against a backdrop of parental stress, and a lack of consistency in parenting styles and philosophies. Georgia appeared to be reacting to her own sense of helplessness in witnessing her parents' behavior. Being of such a young age, she had no coping mechanisms to deal with them, except to act out. We could say that her behavior was one of acting out against the systematic patterns she found herself enmeshed in.

When Maria and James modified their parenting styles and behavior, and practiced mindful parenting, the anxiety and negative emotions Georgia experienced appeared to abate. At the same time, Georgia was able to regulate her emotions when her parents started to regulate their own emotions. In working with families, the therapist should not focus too much on which family member is the "presenting patient," or who needs therapy first. I usually adopt the approach of counseling one family member but encouraging the whole family to participate in the exercises and tasks I assign to the client I am seeing. I know that, invariably, the whole family will benefit.

The approach I had taken with Maria, Georgia, and their family is informed by systems therapy, also known as the systematic therapy approach.[35] Briefly, in this kind of therapy, relationships and interactions between family members, and the way these interactions entangle and impact on the family as a whole, are explored and discussed. Systems therapy works with the whole family organically. This is because when one part of the system shifts, the rest of the system moves and adjusts as well.

We see a good example of this systematic approach in the role-modeling of appreciation and gratitude. When I explained to Georgia the rationale of "giving with both hands," Georgia intuitively understood and practiced this with her family. And the behavior she role-modeled was in turn followed by her parents. As Maria put it, "We are in a better rhythm now."

There is a Buddhist teaching called "Indra's net."[36] Indra's net comprises a large net of jewels, each of which reflects and is reflected by all the other jewels in the net, demonstrating that everything in the universe is interrelated. It is a powerful analogy for interconnectedness. Indra's net is also a good metaphor for family systems where each family member reflects and is reflected by the others. Such was the case with Georgia and her family.

Many clinicians are familiar with and use system therapy in their counseling. Many parents may not. However, you might find it helpful to apply this idea in your engagement with your kids. As we witnessed in my counseling with Georgia, when her parents were stressed or anxious, Georgia absorbed their negativity and displayed similar behavior. When her parents moderated their behavior, Georgia moderated her responses as well. The converse also happens – when Georgia was calmer, her parents were less reactive themselves and with the kids.

The analogy I give is that when one car wheel turns, the rest of the vehicle usually align itself to accommodate the turning wheel. I encourage you to role-model behaviors that do not impact negatively on your kids directly or indirectly so, that like the car, the whole family moves in harmony.

Practice Guide

- Empower your kids by role-modeling positive behaviors to them. Be mindful of opportunities, whether big or small, to do so.

- Encourage your children to act as a role model to others. This will enhance their leadership skills and self-confidence.

- Encourage your kids to learn about and express gratitude, appreciation, and respect. Practice gratitude and appreciation to your child yourself.

- Help your family members appreciate and understand the interconnectedness between them. Encourage your children to act in ways that bring about positive responses from the people they interact with.

Chapter 15

WORKING WITH CHALLENGING KIDS

Playing ignorant

"For someone my mother's age, you are quite clever."

– Elizabeth

Working with kids can be a joy and a challenge. It is especially challenging to counsel young clients encountering complicated familial dynamics and complex issues, and who are generally resistant to coming to therapy. Such was the case with Elizabeth, aged 13. In this chapter and Chapter 16, I share some of my counseling work with Elizabeth.

Elizabeth's mother, Rosalind, had referred her for counseling with me. She dropped Elizabeth off after school for her first session and went back to work. Elizabeth sat down, looking bored, folded her arms across her chest, and tucked her legs under the chair. She rejected my offer of a drink and just stared at me defiantly.

"Elizabeth," I asked, "do you know why you are here today? Is there anything that you would like to share with me?"

"I don't know," she muttered. "Ask my mother. She was the one who ordered me to come and paid for my session. I DON'T want to be here. I am okay. I can deal

"Ask my mother. She was the one who ordered me to come. I DON'T want to be here."

with my own problems. I have done that all my life. I don't need people."

I discerned from her body language and defiant tone that a more unconventional approach was called for, and that I needed to establish an early rapport with her in order to break down some of her defenses.

The three options strategy

"It sounds like you don't really want to see me and came because Mum paid for your session," I said. "So, how about I give you a few options. We could sit here quietly, and you don't have to talk. Or you could keep scrolling through your mobile phone until your mum picks you up. Or I could make the first 10 minutes of our session free. If you still don't like us working together, your mum doesn't have to pay for it. The 10 minutes will be on the house. Would you like to give that a try?"

Elizabeth was taken aback by my unusual offer. She eyed me suspiciously.

"Why would you want to do that? No one has given me a freebie before. Everyone wants something."

I smiled.

"Oh, I don't know," I replied nonchalantly. "Because I am generous. Because I like you. Because I think that it's good to share what's bothering us. Take your pick."

Elizabeth still looked hesitant, but she appeared intrigued by my offer. I could sense her body language relaxing. She unfolded her arms and pulled her legs out.

"Okay, I will give it a try. Ten minutes of free counseling. Mum would never believe that," she said.

During the "free" counseling time I encouraged Elizabeth to share her concerns. I learned that her parents had been divorced since she was a baby and that both parents had remarried. Elizabeth lived with her mother, stepfather, and an older sister, Joan. She visited her father and stepmother in the school holidays. I also learned that in the last few years, Elizabeth had been experiencing significant psychological issues including self-harming, depression, anxiety, and rebelliousness. She was defiant with both sets of parents and fought constantly with Joan, whom she had previously got on well with.

Elizabeth was a bright student who excelled in most of her subjects at school. But in the past two years, her grades had dropped significantly. She broke many school rules and had been acting out. As a result, she was often sent to detention class. She had been expelled from her two previous schools and was now enrolled at a third one. Elizabeth informed me that she had been taking an antidepressant for one year, and would like to stop, as the medication made her "feel like a zombie."

"Wow," Elizabeth said, catching her breath after she recounted her list of concerns. "I didn't realize I had so many problems and was able to talk about them so freely. Your listening to me quietly made me able to talk about them easily."

"Thank you for sharing, Elizabeth," I said, "I'm so glad that you were able to. How do you feel?"

"Good," she replied.

"Please tell me more," I said.

"For someone my mother's age, you are quite clever," Elizabeth said. "You knew that I probably couldn't resist a free gift. So I took up your offer. It's like the three options I gave to Mum when I asked her to let me go out with my friends. I would ask her twice for something that I knew that she wouldn't agree to, and which I didn't really want anyway. Then I gave her a third option. She usually agrees. I knew that would happen. She felt bad about saying 'no' twice, and so would say 'yes' the third time. You just did the same thing."

Elizabeth and I laughed at the coincidence of our strategy, and at being unexpected collaborators.

"Would you like to continue the rest of the counseling that your mother paid for, or would you like more free time?" I asked.

Elizabeth chuckled, "It's okay. We can continue the counseling like Mum asked. She would think it is weird if you don't charge me for the whole hour. But thank you. You are quite a clever psychologist, and a rather nice one."

It was my turn to laugh.

"Thank you, Elizabeth. I am glad you think that."

The rest of the counseling session progressed quite smoothly. Elizabeth agreed to return for further sessions, and we selected some dates. Although I had managed to establish some rapport with her, I realized that, given the complexities of her situation and her trust issues, I would need to reinforce the therapeutic foundation I had built with her as her collaborator.

Playing ignorant

A unique opportunity presented itself unexpectedly. I gave Elizabeth a piece of paper to write down the dates for her future sessions.

"Why don't you just text me a reminder? Then I can see it on my phone," Elizabeth suggested.

It is my policy to encourage clients, including young ones, to take responsibility for their counseling and to record their session dates, rather than rely on reminders. So I decided to play ignorant.

"Sorry, Elizabeth" I said, "I am not good at texting."

Elizabeth laughed and came over to my side of the table.

"I can help you. You put your right finger on the keyboard, and your left finger on the calendar. Easy."

"I can help you," she said. "You put your right finger on the keyboard, and your left finger on the calendar. You enter my mobile number and text me the reminder. See. Easy."

"Thank you for showing me," I said. "Sounds like you are good at texting. I'm not good at it. I find it a bit complicated and daunting. Happy to accept your help. But next time, I would prefer that you write down your own dates. Is that a deal?"

Elizabeth rolled her eyes but agreed. She phoned her mother to pick her up.

"Mum," she said to Rosalind, "the psychologist you sent me to see is so dumb [Elizabeth looked at me and winked]. She doesn't even know how to text. I had to help her. But she made me agree to write the dates on paper in future. It's okay. She is quite nice. I'll come back and see her. She is quite happy to admit that she is dumb at texting. I like that. I can tell her about the dumb things I did."

I was pleased that in role-modeling some unexpected offers and confessing to my "technological ignorance," a guarded teenager such as Elizabeth had gained a sense of safety and reassurance that it's okay not to know everything, to be honest about not knowing, and to accept help.

Psychological Explanations and Key Learnings

With young clients experiencing significant psychological concerns, including mistrust and safety issues, it is crucial to establish an early rapport and set the tone and direction for future counseling. Building a trusting relationship often calls for creative thinking on the part of the therapist. In therapy, there is no how-to manual. Being a mindful therapist,[37] the clinician has to be constantly aware of how and what the client is experiencing and feeling during the session. Elizabeth, who had felt caught up in a tangled web of complex family alliances for most of her life, had developed a "survivor's instinct," and armored herself with a sense of bravado. This was evident in her defiant body language and her initial reluctance to share. I sensed, however, that underneath the bravado was a frightened kid who was probably feeling out of her depth in managing her problems.

As was the case with my other client, Georgia (see Chapters 12 and 13), I had to first gain Elizabeth's confidence and trust by allowing her to make her own decisions. Intuitively, I sensed that I needed to engage with Elizabeth in ways that were differentiated from how she related to other significant adults in her life. Hence, I gave her the three options, which she probably was not expecting from a therapist.

I hit the jackpot when she accepted my third offer of 10 minutes' free counseling and shared the powerful insight: "No one has given me a freebie before. Everyone wants something." The reward came when Elizabeth confessed that she did a similar thing with her mother, knowing that her mother would agree to a third option. In Elizabeth's eyes, my giving her three offers, of which she had to choose one, made me a worthy strategist and partner. I had somehow won her confidence.

The other issue that I sensed with Elizabeth was her difficulty in admitting her problems and asking for help – hence her statements: "I can deal with my own problems. I have done that all my life. I don't need people." My openness in sharing my ignorance about texting, and my willingness to accept her help, appeared to give her a sense of safety in reaching out.

A note of caution. "Playing ignorant" by therapists, parents, or significant others must not be experienced by the recipient as patronizing. Intelligent kids such as Elizabeth, who are survivors, have an instinctive wariness and skepticism about other people's motives and actions. It is important to maintain a delicate balance between being honest and being good-humoredly playful but authentically so. It was fortuitous that I was presented with two genuine opportunities to role-model for Elizabeth.

Working with challenging teenagers who appear to have been traumatized by various life events, and who are struggling to find their place in the family, school, society, and peer groups, calls for the clinician to maintain a beginner's mind – a nonjudgmental, curious attitude about everything that is unfolding in the "here and now" in the therapy room. A nonjudgmental attitude involves maintaining continuous awareness of, for example, body language, tone of voice, silent pauses, and the range of emotions expressed verbally or nonverbally by the client. It is a good strategy for the therapist to be mindful of these nuances, role-play appropriate examples, and assist the client in experiencing, in real time, appropriate ways of responding to different situations.

As a parent, you can generalize and use the approach and skills I adopted with Elizabeth, by practicing mindful communication –

maintaining an open, not-knowing attitude (play ignorant), and listening quietly – when your kids share their experiences and concerns with you. This kind of attitude will give them a sense of being listened to and understood.

It is important for you to establish trust and rapport when your kids first come to talk to you. Teenagers face all kinds of pressure, emotionally and psychologically. This kind of pressure can come from within themselves, or externally from peers, social media and other sources. Listen to them nonjudgmentally and try to resist offering solutions and advice until you have gained their trust and a real understanding. I sometimes encounter parents "hijacking" their kids' stories by saying, for example, "When I was your age, this is what I did." And then the parents would proceed to take over the narrative by telling their kids what they did at that age, and how the kids should emulate them. Usually at this stage, you probably see the teenager's eyes glazing over, and their internal dialogue thinking, "Mum/Dad doesn't really get me."

Teenagers experience many transition points at this stage of their development, as you have seen with Elizabeth. When you have earned their respect and trust, they will learn to treat you with reciprocal respect and trust.

Practice Guide

- Be mindful of kids' feelings about seeing a therapist and allow them to make an informed decision.

- Provide a sense of safety for children who are defensive that allows them to share deep concerns openly and freely.

- Use humor to build a trusting relationship with kids.

- Role-play to kids that it is all right to ask for and accept help.

- Be open to sharing and learning from children collaboratively.

Chapter 16

THE BLACK SHEEP
OF THE FAMILY

A label or a strategy?

**"I could be like the black sheep of the family.
That would be like my identity."**

– Elizabeth

Elizabeth was a 13-year-old schoolgirl whom I had been counseling for several months. In Chapter 15, I wrote about my first session with her, and how I used an innovative approach to build trust with her. Elizabeth's biological parents had been divorced since she was a baby. Elizabeth lived with her mother Rosalind, her stepfather Brian, and her older sister Joan, and visited her father and his family during the school holidays. Elizabeth had been acting out at school and was currently studying at her third school, after being expelled from the previous two schools for breaking too many rules. She was experiencing high levels of stress, anxiety, and depression, for which she was taking medication, and she was self-harming.

As our counseling progressed, I learned more about the major problems that Elizabeth was experiencing and that appeared to impact adversely on her mental health. There had many court cases between her biological parents for custody of her and her sister. She constantly clashed with her mother, stepfather, and sister. Elizabeth was also experiencing major trust issues with her father and stepmother.

From these sessions, what stood out for me most was discovering the creative strategies that Elizabeth had devised and implemented to cope. The most notable ones she used were differentiation – rebelling and playing the role of "the black sheep" of the family – and expanding her sense of self by finetuning her given name, Elizabeth.

In this chapter, I discuss these two compelling strategies, as I believe that they demonstrate the complex and creative person Elizabeth is, and her self-awareness about why and how she used each technique as a coping mechanism. I have quoted Elizabeth's explanations extensively, as they show her sensitive nature and how well she was able to express her thoughts and emotions. I also discuss how I worked with Elizabeth mindfully to help her get in touch her emotions and feelings and to make more positive choices.

Differentiation, rebellion, and being the "Black Sheep"

According to Elizabeth, Joan was perceived by their mother to be the good daughter. So, Elizabeth tried to differentiate herself from Joan. It was quite apparent from our discussions that Elizabeth's attempts at differentiation involved rebelling and playing the role of "the black sheep" of the family.

"Joan and I grew up together and people think that we have the same interests," Elizabeth explained. "But we are different ... I'm trying to show everyone that I am different. Like getting my nose pierced. ... I think that the first step is making myself realize that although I'm similar to Joan, we are not the same ... And then making other people see that. Like I am unique ... And when my mum and dad or anyone tries to compare me with my sister, I would say, 'Guess what? I am a different person.'"

"Does it help to see yourself as unique?" I asked.

"Ya. Ya."

I sensed that one possible factor contributing to Elizabeth's depression was her wanting to be her own person but also needing her family's support. Elizabeth agreed.

"I want to be independent, but I don't want to be alone. That's why I get depressed."

"Can you explain how that might that cause you to be depressed?" I asked.

Rebelling to differentiate

"It's like a conflict between who you are," Elizabeth replied. "It's really hard to find a happy medium. Do I want to be the same person I always was, be surrounded by family who is taking a long time to figure out you are no longer wanting to be little ... They are still figuring out that I don't want a little girl's handbag for my birthday."

"I was wondering why that would make you depressed. Why not just rebel?"

"I DID. Ya. I was rebellious."

"Tell me more about that," I said.

"I wanted to be IN trouble," Elizabeth replied. "So that I could be like the black sheep of the family. That would be like my identity when I was growing up. Even though I am moving on past that stage, I'm still called the black sheep. At school, and at home. I have like the biggest attitude problem. I would lie to my mum, and I would go out and do stuff. I would purposely do things that would piss people off."

"Why is that?"

"I don't know. It's a stage that I was going through I suppose. Put on a ton of makeup. Short skirts. I got grounded a lot."

"That is interesting," I said. "I'm curious whether that is being creative or —"

"Or wrong," Elizabeth interjected. She laughed.

Why did you say, 'Or wrong'?"

"I don't know. It just came out."

"Sounds like you saying that you set out to create an identity so that people can relate to you differently from Joan."

"I think that it came naturally because I had so much anger inside of me," Elizabeth said. "And the attitude problem came easily too. The thing is, it really helped me move away from being compared to Joan. Because she is the one who has been really good at school. She got into some trouble at home, but she never really got into trouble at school. ... I think that it did give me an identity because it worried my parents so much. But it was better than not even being thought about. Like, Joan's fine, that means that Elizabeth's fine. It was going to be like 'My God, Elizabeth, stop getting in trouble.' School would call up my mum, and she would talk to my father. It gave me something to go by. I didn't really have to work for that identity because it came easily. But it helped me to sort of move on from that to my real identity."

"And your real identity being?" I asked.

"I'm not really sure," Elizabeth said hesitantly. "I haven't really found it yet. Right now, I'm beginning to be at the mature stage where I think I can comprehend things better. It's overlapping the stage where I was at, the rebellious one."

"It sounds like you saying that it was better to get some negative attention than no attention?"

"Yes," Elizabeth replied without hesitation.

"That is quite clever."

Elizabeth laughed.

"Why didn't you just try and be better than Joan?" I asked.

Elizabeth grinned sheepishly.

"If I did do that, I would be no different from Joan. If I was to be good, then Mum would say, 'Oh my children are so smart and so good.' Because if Joan got an A in English and I got an A in English, she would say that 'they are so smart.' But if I got the total opposite, like really bad reports from all my teachers and go to detention classes often, she would say 'Joan is so good, but Elizabeth is freaking me out.' The thing is, I didn't think that I was going to change my image. It kind of happened gradually. Like, I started speaking back to the teachers, and gradually let my uniform fall apart."

"It sounded like you tried to differentiate yourself so that your parents know that you exist," I said.

"Yes."

"They are aware of you because they had to worry about you constantly?"

Elizabeth looked a bit sad as she responded.

"Yup. They at least have an emotional reaction to me. Which is anger or worry. Before, it was nothing. I'm going past that stage. I am almost past. Like, I still have my little rebellious stuff, and I have a little attitude problem. Dark eyeliner and miniskirts, but they [the miniskirts] are getting longer. A little bit." She laughed. "Little changes. I think that if I didn't change when I changed school, I would be in the shits with my dad. My dad threatened to stop paying my school fees if I didn't."

I offered another view.

"Now that you said that you are moving into this more mature stage, and you are calmer, sweeter, and more understanding, don't you worry that they may not notice you?"

The black sheep strategy

In our discussions, Elizabeth had disclosed that while things had improved, her occasional rule-breaking at her new school still got her into trouble.

"First I was a baby," she replied, "then I was the black sheep. Now I am in between the black sheep and the mature stage. I still get into trouble at school, but not as much trouble. And I am getting good reports from my teachers, but I still get some detention for being late. I don't know what will happen when they get used to me being mature. I guess I'll take on another role," – she laughed – "perhaps Gothic. But I want to do better and not get into trouble so much."

Her expressed wish to want to do better and to not get into so much trouble provided a wonderful opportunity for me to work with her creatively. As in Chapter 15, I realized that I had to come up with a unique strategy of my own – one that would appeal to Elizabeth's sense of "competitiveness" while allowing her to differentiate and to maintain her sense of identity and autonomy. In Chapter 15, I described how Elizabeth had used the strategy of offering her mother three options when she wanted to go out with her friends, knowing that her mother would pick the third option. I decided to use an analogous approach again.

The 3 options strategy again

I threw her a challenge.

"I could offer you three options. The first, you can continue to break school rules and go to detention class. The second, you can continue to rebel at school and at home and be seen as the black sheep. The third option – I was thinking that it is actually quite easy to break school rules. Any student can really do that. I think that it's harder to follow the school rules and not get into trouble."

Elizabeth responded as I suspected she would.

"I can do the third one. Follow school rules, I mean. Easy."

We agreed that she would try to follow the school rules for two weeks, and also try not get into trouble at home.

At the next counseling session, Elizabeth reported that she had not broken any rules and had not got into trouble.

"That's good," I said, "but I think that two weeks is easy for a bright student like you. Can you keep out of trouble for, say, two months?"

"Two months. Easy. You are on," Elizabeth replied.

In the follow-up sessions, Elizabeth showed she had kept her end of the agreement, and I kept extending the period of good behavior. It was a pleasant surprise when Elizabeth happily reported her success and looked to me at each session to extend the timeline. We continued doing so for six months, at the end of which Elizabeth was not breaking rules or getting into trouble, even without an agreement.

I learned about the surprising success of my approach when her mother Rosalind came in one day to pay Elizabeth's bills.

"Elizabeth is doing really well at school," she told me. "Her grades have all gone up, and she is excelling at all her subjects. Her father is really pleased with her results. She followed all the school rules, wore her school uniform at the prescribed length, and discarded her makeup and 'crazy' hairdo. She is nicer to all the family members. I didn't have to ground her even once. She seemed to be happier, calmer, less depressed, and less stressed. It's funny. Whenever she asked me for something, she gave me three alternatives. Why do you think she is doing that? How did you help my daughter?"

Listening to Rosalind's account, I smiled.

"That's great to know. I am glad to hear that things are working out well for everyone, especially for Elizabeth."

Good on you, Elizabeth, I thought to myself, *The three options strategy. Works every time.* Naturally, I did not share with Rosalind the rationale for Elizabeth's strategy. It remained confidential between Elizabeth and me as collaborators.

"Rosalind," I said, "Your daughter is an intelligent, highly creative person. All I did was to trust her, and appeal to her sense of integrity and fair play. And I helped her to realize that being a strong, positive teenager, is better than being the 'black sheep' of the family."

Rosalind nodded.

"I agree. She is a much nicer person to be around."

Expanding her sense of self: Finetuning Elizabeth's given name

Another interesting strategy which Elizabeth adopted was to finetune her given name from Elizabeth to Eliza and then Liza. She used this approach to expand her sense of self, to represent how she felt about herself at various stages, and how she wished other people to perceive and relate to her.

I was curious. "Why was it so important for you to adjust your name as you grew up?"

"I like the name Liza better than Eliza," she explained. "That was what everyone called me when I was little. It is SUCH a young name. My friends now call me Liza. I think that it's really cool. When I was young, I got called Eliza. But now I am a teenager, and even when I am 20 or something, I will get called Liza. … Dad realized it, but it's hard for him to get used to it. Like, he would call me 'Eliza' and say 'Oh, sorry, sorry,' and then he would call me Liza. Yes. I think that some of it might be about not letting me grow up. I like my name to be Liza and people confuse it with Eliza. It is definitely Liza."

I smiled at Elizabeth's well-crafted rationale.

"When I'm old, I shall be called Elizabeth again," she continued.

I stifled a laugh. "Sounds like you are planning to change your name again?"

"Ya, when I'm old. When you are old, you can't be called Eliza."

"When will you allow yourself to be called Elizabeth?"

"When I feel the time is right. Like when I get my first gray hair. Like when I have gone past my party stage. Grown up, married or something."

I was amazed at how much thought Elizabeth had put into her plan for expanding her sense of self through finetuning her name. It would appear she had considered the rationale and purpose from all angles and had taken steps to introduce this strategy to her friends and family, gradually but firmly. Best of all, I liked her sense of humor when she described her exasperation at her parents' reactions. It was obvious she took the refinement of her name seriously but regarded other people's oversight with amusement.

At the end of our session, Elizabeth showed me the assessment for her English assignment, where she had topped the class. She said she was doing well at school and enjoying all her subjects. Elizabeth said she had told her class coordinator that she was depressed and had been taking antidepressants, and that she was now seeing a psychologist and doing better. Elizabeth also indicated that she had no current or outstanding concerns. We agreed that it would be a good time to finish counseling.

"Thank you for all your help, Belinda," Elizabeth said, looking happy but a bit tearful. "I'm so much more comfortable with myself and with others. I appreciate all your help."

"You are very welcome, Elizabeth," I replied. "I've enjoyed working with you very much. I have learned a lot from you. Especially about the three options strategy."

Elizabeth was visibly pleased and grinned.

"You are a beautiful, wonderful person," I told her, "and you will grow up to be a wonderful woman."

Psychological Explanations and Key Learnings

Working with Elizabeth, someone so young but highly intelligent and self-aware, was very rewarding. She is someone I would describe as an "adult in transition." I was particularly admiring of how she had managed and coped with her childhood experiences and traumas before she came to counseling. As I worked with Elizabeth, two metaphors came to mind.

The first is that she is like a fledgling – the term for a baby bird that has grown out of its flight feathers and is preparing for life in the outside world. The baby bird is ready to leave the nest but still relies on its parents for food and shelter. The metaphor of the fledging came to mind when Elizabeth wistfully said, "I want to be independent, but I don't want to be alone. That's why I get depressed." So, like a fledging, Elizabeth kept circling the nest, moving in and out, wanting autonomy and independence but still scared of leaving home without familial support. This is the reality of a teenager in transition, as Elizabeth was – idealistic, passionate, yet vulnerable.

The second metaphor that came to mind is that of "Spring kid," the theme of this book. The term SPRING is used as an analogy for the season of spring and a spring device. Elizabeth appeared to display some of the qualities of a spring. This kind of mechanism has significant shock-absorbent qualities – it can be taut and stiff at times, and at other times flexible, with the ability to stretch under applied pressure. When Elizabeth first narrated her problems, she seemed like a coiled spring, tight and unyielding. At the same time, she appeared to be able to stretch herself under external pressure and not fall apart. When she explained how she had managed her problems to date, and responded well to my counseling advice, she demonstrated her ability to be flexible and to bounce back to her more positive self.

As a parent, if you are engaging with a child who at times seems like a fledgling and a spring mechanism, like Elizabeth, you will encounter interesting and special challenges for which it would be helpful for you to adopt a mindful approach. For example, if I had asked Elizabeth "Why?" or "Why did you do that?" she would probably have become defensive and coiled into her shell again. I recommend instead that you try to empathize and understand what your child is trying to share with you. Inquire with curiosity; for example, say, "It sounds like you are saying/feeling/thinking …" or simply, "Tell me more." In this way, you can check in with what your kid is trying to communicate and respond appropriately – the idea of respond-ability that I discussed in Chapter 5.

Additionally, if I had sounded disbelieving or patronizing, Elizabeth would have retreated into the nest like a fledging and moved away. By adopting a nonjudgmental stance with Elizabeth, I was able to support her and reinforce her sense of autonomy in making her own decisions and choices.

When Elizabeth's mother Rosalind informed me that Elizabeth was doing well, she asked, "How did you help my daughter?" The mindful approach I took with Elizabeth is one I would highly recommend you adopt when you interact with intelligent, sensitive kids, especially teenagers.

I learned a lot from Elizabeth, not only about her traumas but also about her creative solutions. The most compelling strategy I learned from Elizabeth, and used tactically myself, was the three options solution. I also learned that Elizabeth used the idea of being "the black sheep" both as a label and a strategy to get her family to acknowledge her.

I recommend listening mindfully to your kids. You will be surprised at how much you will learn.

Practice Guide

- Be mindful of the strategies and coping mechanisms (explicit and implicit) used by kids to manage their problems.

- Be nonjudgmental and curious about what information is being shared. Ask open-ended rather than closed questions; for example, "Tell me more" rather than "Why?"

- Discuss the coping strategies used by your kids. Try to use similar techniques with them.

- Understand your children and role-play exercises that appeal to their nature; for example, how I engaged with Elizabeth's keen sense of competitiveness.

- Set aside your ego. Acknowledge what you have learned from the kids. Your acknowledgment will reinforce their self-confidence and self-belief.

Chapter 17

"AM I A SNAKE?"

Exploring self-identity: Learnings from animal friends

"Who am I and what is my name?"

– Li-Kai

It was a bright, sunny morning on January 29, 2025. Another Lunar New Year had begun, marking the birthday of wood snake.

Continuing the tradition of honoring the birth of water tiger (2022), water rabbit (2023), and wood dragon (2024), this chapter celebrates the birth of wood snake.[38] I write about wood snake's friendship with his animal friends, and how the animals helped him discover himself in a fictionalized counseling session.

Snake's journey of self-exploration

Baby snake was born in the lunar year of the green wood element. Moving quietly in the field of yellow spring flowers, he looked down at his green scales and was feeling a bit lost and confused.

"Who am I?" he wondered. There was no one to ask.

Suddenly, out of the grass, three zodiac animal friends appeared: Pi-Hu (water tiger), Mei-Mei (water rabbit), and Shan-Long (wood dragon). The friends greeted him.

"Who am I?"

"Happy birthday, baby snake," they called out. "We brought you a pair of red socks for good luck."

"Thank you," baby snake whispered shyly. "Can you please tell me who or what I am?

"We think you are a wood snake," Pi-Hu, Mei-Mei, and Shan-Long replied. "But we can take you to see a friendly psychologist, Dr. Belinda Khong, who will be able to tell you for sure who you are, and what kind of a snake you are."

"I would like that," snake replied, "But I'm scared."

"Don't be," the animal friends assured him. "We'll go with you as your peer support group."

Snake in counseling

Holding on to Pi-Hu and Mei-Mei, snake sat on Shan-Long's back and the four animal friends flew to Belinda's office. As they walked into the office, Pi- Hu jumped straight onto the couch, lay down, and extended one of his paws. It was obvious that he had been in counseling with Belinda before and was quite comfortable in the therapy room Snake, Mei-Mei, and Shan-Long sat facing Pi-Hu and Belinda.

"So, Doc," Pi-Hu said aloud. "There I was in the middle of the jungle, lost my stripes and I had absolutely no idea who I was. You helped me discover that I'm a water tiger. Can you do the same thing for my snake friend here?"

"So, Doc, I lost my stripes and had no idea who I was.
You helped me discover that I am a water tiger.
Can you help my snake friend here?"

Belinda smiled and nodded. Facing baby snake, she extended her hand to him.

"Hi, I am Belinda. I'm a psychologist. What's your name?"

"I have no idea. Who am I and what is my name?" Baby snake looked sad. "Can you help me?"

"You are a wood snake," Belinda replied.

"I AM a snake? Can you tell me more?"

"Well, you are born in 2025, and you are the sixth animal in the Chinese 12-year zodiac cycle, following the Year of the Wood Dragon in 2024. You will be followed by the Year of the Horse in 2026."

"I would like to have a name," baby snake said. "Can you please give me one? A beautiful, meaningful name like my friends have?"

"Of course," Belinda replied. "How would you like to be called Li-Kai 丽凯? It is a Chinese name meaning 'beautiful victory.'"

"Why do you call me Li-Kai?" baby snake asked.

"The Chinese character or radical *li* 丽 means 'beautiful' and comprises the stroke, one 一, meaning that you are unique, one of a kind. The radicals 朋 are the symbols for a pair of reindeer's antlers, meaning 'balanced' or 'in harmony.'

"The Chinese word *kai* 凯 means victory or triumph. It comprises the word 山, representing the mountain. The character 己 means 'oneself,' and the character 几 means 'several.' So the name Kai is a metaphor for someone who has a positive attitude and is able to climb mountains and overcome many challenges if they are strong, balanced, and brave."

"I like that. But I am only a baby snake."

"Yes, you are little," Belinda said, "but if you live like your name Li-Kai, it means that you are beautiful and unique. You are also brave and can overcome obstacles, in similar way to climbing a mountain.

"Your name Li-Kai also shares many of the meanings in your animal friends' name."

"Can you explain that?" Li-Kai asked.

"Well, water tiger was called Pi-Hu, meaning 'brave tiger.' Water rabbit was called Mei-Mei, meaning 'beautiful little sister.' And wood dragon was called Shan-Long, meaning mountain dragon.' So all your friends' names are in your name."

"Hurrah. Cool!" Li-Kai exclaimed. "My name also has my mummy's Chinese name, Li, in it. Now I know it means 'beautiful.'"

Belinda was happy to see the joy on Li-Kai's face.

Snake's self-understanding and self-acceptance

"Li-Kai. Welcome to our animal world." Pi-Hu, Mei-Mei and Shan-Long rushed out and hugged Li-Kai. He hugged them back, delighted to learn that he is a beautiful, brave snake from the mountain, and that he is accepted by his peer group. But he still looked a bit sad.

"But ... but ... people don't like snakes. They said that I'm ugly and scary. People run away when they see me."

Pi-Hu roared and jumped up from the couch.

"Li-Kai, people don't like me either. They think I will eat them. But only when I am hungry, hahaha!" Pi-Hu laughed at his own joke.

"People are scared of me too," Shan-Long said. "They think I'm not a real animal. They keep drawing funny pictures of me. I look better than their drawings. They should use AI to generate nicer pictures!" Shan-Long laughed at his own joke too.

"Li-Kai, people like me," Mei-Mei said quietly. "They think that I'm cute. But they want to take me home and keep me as a pet. They kept feeding me carrots. I HATE carrots."

Mei-Mei pretended to look annoyed. All the animal friends chuckled at her comments.

Belinda joined in the commentary with a cheeky smile.

"Li-Kai, I was also born in the Year of the Tiger, like Pi-Hu. I'm sure all my animal and human clients are scared of me. They never stay around here for long!"

The animal friends roared with laughter and delight.

"Thank you for sharing your stories," Li-Kai said, looking relieved. "I like that I'm not scary, just different. It doesn't seem to worry you all what others think of you. I will learn not to worry too. We are all beautiful in our own ways."

Belinda was pleased by the empathy and understanding Li-Kai had received from his animal peers. Everyone sharing about how others reacted to them seemed to reassure Li-Kai. Moreover, the animals' ability to tell their stories with a sense of humor and to demonstrate self-acceptance appeared to reduce Li-Kai's anxiety about being accepted. Belinda was also happy to see that Li-Kai was able to reframe his self-description from "I am ugly" to "I am different," and to conclude that "We are all beautiful in our own ways."

"Li-Kai, contrary to popular belief," Belinda added, "in Chinese culture, as a snake, you represent wisdom. You are considered to be intelligent and wise. You have refined taste but can be quite mysterious and enigmatic. You are regarded as a great thinker with good intuition. And you possess good leadership skills and a strong determination to reach your goals. Some famous snake people include President Xi JinPing, President John F. Kennedy, Stephen Hawking, J. K. Rowling and Prince George."

Li-Kai clapped his hands. "I like that. I am cool!"

All his animal friends clapped their hands in excitement too. "Li-Kai, you are awesome," they said.

Li-Kai smiled enigmatically.

At the end of the counseling session, the four animal friends skipped and danced out of my office.

Riding on Shan-Long's back,

Pi-Hu sat on his left wing,

Doing his thing.

Mei-Mei sat on his right wing,

Throwing carrots away with a zing,

Li-Kai sat in between,

Looking happy and serene.

They looked a sight, but what a beautiful sight! A group of animals who had discovered and accepted themselves for how and who they are.

If only my human clients were as insightful, and kind to themselves and others, Belinda reflected wistfully. Maybe, one day my animal clients can counsel my human ones. She smiled at her own joke, as the animal friends had taught her.

Psychological Explanations and Key Learnings

This charming story about wood snake, who became known as Li-Kai, reflects many of the concerns that kids experience growing up in the world. Questions such as "Who am I?" and "What am I?" abound. Issues about self-understanding, self-acceptance, and acceptance by their peers constantly trouble my young clients.

The fictional counseling story about the birth of wood snake can be used as an aid by therapists and parents to help children explore and normalize their own feelings about self-identity and self-understanding. The actions and behavior of the animal friends, the illustrations, and the humor in the chapter demonstrate how a group therapy with peers who can offer understanding, empathy, and compassion provides important psychological learnings for young people. Equally valuable is helping kids learn to reframe their self-beliefs and to refine their thinking about their own limitations and strengths.

As a parent, you can encourage your child to talk about their feelings by sharing simple, interesting stories with them. The psychological strategies and mindful therapeutic approach I outline here are easy to put in place with your kids if you use creativity and humor to work with them. You can adapt the wood snake story to use with your child with the following practice guide.

Practice Guide

- Be sensitive to your children's concerns about self-identity, self-understanding, self-acceptance, and peer acceptance.

- Use interesting, illustrative stories such as "Am I a snake?" as play exercises to encourage your kids to discuss and explore similar feelings.

- Role-play with your kids and discuss which animal's experiences they identify with.

- Explore with your kids what they have learned about how the animals resolve their problems, and how they can use these insights to help themselves.

- Help your children focus on what is good and positive about themselves, such as through the meaning of their names, as wood snake did.

- Encourage peers and family members to offer compassion, empathy, and support to your kids, as the animal friends showed to wood snake.

Part 4

Guide for Nurturing Mindful Kids

In Parts 1–3, you have read about raising a Spring kid, how to use the wisdom from the Buddha's teachings and the animal friends' advice to kids, and how to apply the counseling approach I use with my young clients when engaging with kids.

Part 4 rounds off my psychological guide on how to nurture mindful kids, focusing on building your skills in mindful parenting. In Chapter 18, I have compiled some of the most effective tips for you to use. Chapter 19 offers some sample practice exercises and explanations from the drawings of kids and parents, for you to learn how to communicate with kids through pictures. And in Chapter 20, I show how you can support Spring kids to become Great kids. The illustration shows myself, my illustrator Pip, and the artists (kids and parents) who appear in Chapter 19 enjoying ourselves in the art studio.

Savour the joy and fun of nurturing mindful kids.

By the end of Part 4, whether you are a parent, clinician, educator, healthcare professional, or caregiver working with kids, you will have learned how to:

- use the skills and techniques I provide to communicate effectively with kids of varying ages
- use the themes, discussions, exercises, and practices to help your child to become a Spring and Great kid.
- use the psychological explanations and key learnings to gain a greater understanding of your kids and how to work with them in a range of contexts.
- provide your kids with a set of positive values and life skills that can help them cope with different emotional and psychological challenges.

Chapter 18

TIPS FOR NURTURING MINDFUL KIDS

Parenting, like a river, is a journey, not a destination.
Each river has its own story to tell, so does each
parent-child relationship.

Welcome to the continuing journey of *Raising Spring Kids*. In Part 1, I used the analogy of the spring tree as a metaphor for the growth of a child. In this chapter, I use the analogy of a river for parenting.

Like a river, parenting is a journey rather than a destination. Each river has its own unique story to tell; as does each parent–child relationship. A river rushes over rocks, develops into cascading waterfall over steep rocky ledges, or meanders gently in still estuaries, carefully navigating and adapting to the twists and curves of its terrain. Similarly, the parenting journey is a continual process of excitement, adventures, challenges, and sometimes just plain sailing. The journey in this book is intended to support you and your kids to navigate the terrain as skillfully as possible.

Parenting, like a river, is a journey. Each river has its own story to tell, so does each parent-child relationship.

In this chapter, I offer some practical tips, advice, recommendations, and exercises for you to learn essential skills for working with your kids. The tips offered in this section can be likened to oars. An oar is a simple pole that is designed to help the rower steer the boat attentively. The effectiveness of the oar depends on the user's efforts to try out, refine, and practice using it. In the same way, the skills and tips are useful when you apply them regularly so that they become instinctive and natural to use.

From working with families and kids for decades, the most important tips and skills I recommend are the following:

- Practice mindful communication.
- Ask open-ended questions.
- "Resist fixing": Offer clear choices and boundaries.
- Be the best positive role model you can be.

I have set out the advice and examples in a way that is simple and easy for you to follow. I will also refer back to some of the tips and skills that have already been discussed in earlier chapters, as a reminder of their importance. You might like to print out the advice and illustrations as daily reminders and flashcards, to use for further discussions.

Practice mindful communication

When engaging with your kids, it is important for you to practice mindful communication. This involves:

- cultivating a beginner's mind – "not-knowing," open, and receptive
- quiet listening – reducing your internal dialogue and rumination
- being nonjudgmental, avoiding preconceptions, beliefs, and ideas.

Practice mindful communication.

The following is a condensed version of a well-known classic Zen story, "Empty your cup," which captures many of these tips and skills.

Empty your cup[39]

High in the mountain, there lived a Zen master and teacher who was renowned for his wisdom. One day a scholar, who was proud of his own knowledge of and opinions about Zen, visited the teacher and asked to learn more about Zen. The master agreed and invited the scholar to first join him for a cup of tea. The master kept pouring tea into the cup until it overflowed and spilled on the table.

"Master, the cup is full, and no more tea can go in!" the scholar exclaimed.

The master paused.

"You are like the teacup," he said, "full of your own ideas and opinions about Zen. To really learn, you must first empty your cup."

The scholar understood the lesson: that if he really wanted to find out more about Zen teachings, he must first empty his mind, free himself from preconceptions, beliefs, and opinions, and listen quietly.

The key message from the story is the importance of emptying your "mental teacup" in order to:

- cultivate an open and receptive mind, so that you can absorb what is being communicated by your child
- be willing to let go of any preconceived notions and ideas that may cloud your judgment
- be open to learning about your kid's concerns, perspectives, and experiences directly from them
- practice humility and recognize that there is always more to learn and discover about your child, and that you may not have all the answers.

An empty teacup is a good analogy for the attitude you can adopt when communicating with your kids. You will then be able to really understand your child's perspectives and appreciate what they are trying to share. Through mindful communication, you may also discover that you do not necessarily have all the answers and should avoid offering quick solutions.

**Cultivate quiet listening – empty your mind,
like an empty teacup.**

In Chapters 7 and 8, I recommended a range of exercises and practice guides to promote mindful communication. I encourage you to revisit these chapters for useful examples and key learnings on cultivating this approach.

Ask open-ended rather than close-ended questions

Open-ended questions are questions that produce more than a one-word response. This type of question invites the other person to share their thoughts, feelings, and experiences in a deeper way; to explore possibilities; and to bring forth more information. On the other hand, closed-ended questions usually produce a simple, monosyllabic "Yes" or "No" response that effectively closes down the conversation.

To complement mindful communication, you should strive to keep closed-ended questions to a minimum – perhaps just at the start of the conversation – and to employ more open-ended questions during the actual exchange. Some important benefits of open-ended questions include facilitating your kids to:

- expand their communication and language skills
- use their imagination and creativity in responding
- enhance social relationships with reciprocal questions and answers.

Examples of closed-ended and open-ended questions.

Open-ended questions can be adjusted depending on the age of your child. The following are some tips and examples of how you can use open-ended questions.

- Use "how," "what," "why," "when," and "who":

    "How do you feel?"

    "What do you think happens next?

    "Why are you feeling sad/anxious/stressed?"

    "When did you find out about that?"

    "Who helped you with that problem?"

- Use open-ended questions to help your kids re
    as opportunities for learning:

    "How would you do it differently next time?"

    "What did you learn from your actions?" (see Chapter 3)

- Start open-ended questions with an inquiry:

    "I wonder if you can show me … ?"

    "Is there another way to … ?"

    "It sounds like you are feeling angry … ?"

- Use books, drawings and storytelling as conversation aids:

  "What do you think the book/story/drawing is about?

  "Can you tell me what happened to [name of character in the story]?"

  "How would you feel if you had the same experience?"

- Encourage your kid to use open-ended and follow-up questions to develop conversational skills:

  "How was your work today, Mummy"

  "How was your holiday?"

  "What are you cooking for dinner tonight?"

  "Can I learn to cook with you?"

Using open-ended questions is one of the most effective techniques you can use to check in on your kids' perspectives and make them feel they are being heard and supported. Such questions also invite children to reflect, encouraging them to think for themselves and learn from their own insights. I encourage you to read Chapters 4 and 11–17 again to see how I use open-ended questions with kids and clients, and practice using such questions yourself.

Offer clear, simple choices, and set boundaries

It is important that you allow your kids to work out their own solutions. This means trying to resist the inclination to fix their problems and, at times, the kids themselves, even though your actions may be motivated by love and caring. If you mete out ready-made solutions, your child may lose the motivation and ability to work out alternative options and to cultivate resilience.

So what can you offer instead? When your child seeks your help, set out clear offers, options, and boundaries. Rather than fixing your kids' problems, encourage them to be mindful and take the personal responsibility to:

- evaluate your offers and make an appropriate choice. When my client, Elizabeth expressed her reluctance to come for counseling, I offered her the options of not talking, scrolling through her mobile phone until her mother collected her, or taking up my offer of 10 minutes of free counseling in order to decide whether she wished to work with me. Elizabeth was intrigued by my unusual offers and elected the 10 minutes of free counseling. She continued to see me for a further six months and learned to manage her psychological concerns (see Chapter 15).

- reflect on the practical consequences of the boundaries set. When Gerald habitually threatened to run away from home, his father Michael set clear boundaries by granting Gerald his wish to run away from home while stipulating that in so doing, Gerald would have to stay in a hotel by himself. Gerald exercised his responsibility to stay home when he understood the consequences of what was involved in taking up his father's offer (see Chapter 4).

Be mindful. Make appropriate choices and observe boundaries.

Chapters 5 and 16 provide further examples and discussions on offering clear choices and setting boundaries. It is a good idea to first ask your child some open-ended questions, in order to ascertain relevant information, before making any offers.

Be the best positive role model you can be

A role model can be described as a person who serves as an example to and is at times imitated by others. For most children, their teachers, peers, family members, and parents are their immediate role models. As I have shown in this book, spiritual teachers from the wisdom traditions and animals are also good role models, and everyone can learn from them. You are your child's most influential role model, so in this section I focus on the role of parents.

Children are like sponges. They watch, they listen, and they copy. Children keenly observe their parents' behavior. They make sense of the world and learn languages and behaviors by emulating their parents. In their formative years, kids often repeat parental behavior, sometimes without really understanding the implications of what they are copying. Parental role models can have a positive or negative impact on kids. It is therefore important that you strive to be the best positive role model you can be.

Throughout this book, I have emphasized the significant role you, as a parent, play in the development of your children. I have shown how some parental actions and behavior – for example, giving kids unlimited screen time on television, computers, and social media, or too many toys, or keeping them constantly entertained to avoid boredom – can result in kids being unable to exercise discipline and restraint, not learning to play creatively on their own, and developing a sense of entitlement. This kind of parental action can also be exhausting for both parents and kids, as it often perpetuates a cycle of ceaseless demands for more and more. Some of the rationale I hear from parents are: "I'm tired," "It's easier to just give my children the computer, mobile phone, or the television to amuse themselves," or "I need some personal space, personal time."

Be the best role model you can be.

Like many parents I encounter, you might have the wrong perception that the path of less resistance is less demanding. Paradoxically, positive parental role-modeling can in fact be less exhausting, less expensive, and simpler to organize. The practices and exercises I have recommended in this book are based on activities that are inspired by nature, animals, books, drawings, storytelling, and the kids' own collection of toys. Try them out with your kids. You might also like to try out the following activities as ongoing projects in order to role-model positive values.

The gratitude and good deeds jar

Place a gratitude and good deeds jar in the house. Involve and encourage your family members to drop in stories about the good deeds they have performed, the good things that happened to them, spare change, little gifts, messages of affirmation, or a simple request to help another person in need. The jar can be decorated and labeled, "Contribute to the gratitude and good deeds jar often." You can open the jar weekly when you enjoy quiet time with the family. Read the stories and affirmations out together, and invite each family member to share their insights and learnings from the notes. You can also organize for the monies to be donated to agreed charities, and discuss with your kids ways of helping the people in need who are identified in the jar. I encourage you to vary and adapt this exercise as you wish.

Decluttering and recycling project

While most families engage in recycling and decluttering, these activities are usually undertaken by the older members of the family. I recommend that you involve your kids too. Invite them to decide what they would like to declutter from their possessions (such as toys, books,

Contribute to the gratitude and good deeds jar often.

and clothes) and how they wish to recycle the items. Similar to the kids' reading center activity described in Chapter 5, kids can be given the responsibility of classifying the items according to subject, age, and gender, and placing them in boxes decorated and labeled by the kids themselves. Together, as a family, you can deliver the items to agreed charities and organizations.

Carry out this project quarterly, half-yearly, or around meaningful occasions. The classification, storage, and delivery activity can make the decluttering and recycling project a fun exercise for all, rather than a chore. The project also helps your children learn to take charge and appreciate that decluttering and recycling is good for the environment, the family, and others.

Writing books project

When I decided to write the Lunar New Year animal books to promote positive values for kids (see Introduction), I enlisted my grandsons Matthew and Nicholas and my friends'

Decluttering and recycling is good for the environment, the family and others.

children to help with the books. I discussed with them the storylines, themes, exercises, and illustrations, and incorporated their feedback, recommendations, and insights on how to inspire kids. You can adapt the writing project to suit your child's age and interest.

The tips and projects I have recommended in this chapter are intended as simple aids for you to enjoy your time with your child, while building on your mindful parenting skills. The tips can serve as oars to help you steer the boat along the parenting journey. While the activities do require some time-commitment, imagination, and creativity on your part, they can be fun, inspirational, and worthwhile for the whole family.

**Writing books together provides endless hours
of fun and learnings for all.**

Chapter 19

KIDS AND PARENTS DRAW

Sample practice exercises

**A delightful showpiece of illustrations and stories by
kids and parents reflecting the themes in this book.**

Chapter 19 holds a special place in the book. In this chapter I showcase drawings from kids and parents, and their explanations for their compositions. I hope readers who have enjoyed the inspiring narratives and beautiful illustrations in the book are inspired to try out similar activities as my participants, "the artists," did.

I invited a number of kids and adults to draw and to explain their drawings. I shared with my participants that I was writing my fourth book, and asked them to help me with this special chapter. They all readily agreed. I gave them some paper, crayons, and pens. My instructions were simple:

- Identify the Chinese zodiac animal sign of your year of birth. This information can be easily obtained from the Chinese zodiac calendar (available at the back of this book) and all my Lunar New Year animal books for kids series: *Am I a Tiger?*, *Water Rabbit's Mindful Adventures*, and *Dragon and Friends' Mindful Adventures*.

- Compose a drawing involving your own animal sign and/or other animals.

- Use your imagination. There are no special guidelines or rules for your drawing.

After the drawing was completed, I invited each participant to tell me about their drawing. The younger participants chose their own title and shared their explanations and stories, which I recorded and transcribed. The older participants wrote their own explanations and stories.

The compositions are presented here as:

- the drawing
- the explanation/story
- my observations and comments.

Acey

Acey is aged 4 and was born in the Year of the Rat.

Drawing by Acey.

Acey's explanation: "Shopping for animals"

Once a upon a time, there were two rabbits (called Bunny and Rabbit), one snake (called Snake) and a horse (called Horse). They were looking for food to eat. They are eating carrots and watermelon. Acey went shopping for food, to help them look for food. Acey found carrots and a watermelon and an orange. Acey said, "Eat a little bit. Please share." Mummy is also shopping for food. My sisters, Zoe [aged 9] and Kelsey [aged 7] are helping Mummy to shop. Daddy is working, and not shopping. Popo [Grandma] is doing laundry.

Author's observations and comments

Acey came to my house with her mother Kerry. Kerry had discussed with her the purpose of our visit. I put the request to her again, as I wanted her to make her own decision.

"Acey, would you like to draw a picture for my new book?"

"Yes, please," Acey replied.

I showed her all the three Lunar New Year animal books and the Chinese zodiac calendar. Kerry explained to Acey that she was born in the Year of the Rat, and asked whether she would like to draw that. Acey gave a firm "No." I suspect young children have concerns with rats, which is understandable.

I encouraged Acey to draw whatever she liked. So Acey drew two rabbits, a snake, and a horse, and named them herself. She outlined and colored in the animals and the people. She told the story of the animals looking for food, and how she and her mother and sisters shopped for food for the animals. I was impressed with her advice to the animals to eat sparingly and to share the food – insightful and sensible advice from a 4-year old. Later, Acey asked Kerry to spell out the family members' names, and she wrote them down herself. I was amused by Acey's comments on her father, "working and not shopping," and her grandmother doing laundry. Kerry confirmed that her observations were spot on.

Acey's composition and explanation showed that she is an intelligent, perceptive girl with firm ideas of what she wanted to draw, and the story she wanted to tell. Her explanation also demonstrated her sense of empathy and compassion (shopping for the animals who are looking for food), and giving the animals good advice on eating only what they needed and sharing.

Acey's keen observation of her father and grandmother's home activities, which Kerry was able to confirm as accurate, showed Acey's mindful attention to family life (see Chapter 7). Overall, Acey's contribution shows good evidence of a young child displaying the qualities of a Spring and Great kid (which I will discuss in Chapter 20). In Chapter 1, I noted that all kids are born spiritual, possessing a sense of wonder, curiosity, empathy, and compassion. Acey's practice exercise certainly showed that.

Harrison

Harrison is aged 6 and was born in the Year of the Dog.

Drawing by Harrison.

Harrison's explanation: "Harrison and Harry in the garden"

Once a upon a time, Harrison, his dog Harry, and Harrison's mum Cheryl went to a garden party. They bumped into Anton, Harrison's friend. And then they walked together to see the robots. One of the robots was very big, and it couldn't fit into the robots' room. Harry was climbing up the big robot, called Banana, and he almost fell. Harry said, "Woof." He was at the top of the big robot. And there is a switch. Harry tapped the button with his foot. The big robot turned very small, and Harry got off the robot. The end.

Author's observations and comments

I met Harrison at his house. His grandmother Joyce was looking after him for the day. When I arrived, Harrison had organized all the three Lunar New Year animal books (he owned all three books and read them regularly), some paper, and crayons, ready to draw. Joyce explained that Harrison was looking forward to our project.

"I'm born in the Year of the Dog," Harrison said, "and I want to draw and write a story about Harry, my dog."

Harrison expressed the wish to draw on his own, so Joyce and I had tea and left him to draw. Later Harrison announced, "I'm finished," and showed us his drawing. I invited Harrison to tell me more about his composition, about going to a garden party with Harry and his mother, and meeting his good friend Anton.

The interesting aspect of Harrison's drawing was the way he infused fantasy into his narrative. Harrison's fantasy story was about meeting robots, and in particular a big robot that he amusingly named Banana, which could not fit into the robots' room. Harrison also incorporated drama in his story, describing how Harry climbed up Banana and almost fell. So Harrison came up with the solution of making Harry press a switch with his foot, which shrunk the robot, allowing Harry to get off.

The exercise with Harrison spoke of an intelligent 6-year-old who is highly organized and conscientious (reading the books before my arrival, laying them out, and organizing papers and crayons ready for our exercise). He also displayed significant independence by asking to draw on his own and letting us know when he was finished.

One of the more intriguing details was how Harrison introduced drama into his story, and his solution for getting his dog Harry down from the tall robot. Harrison's creative use of a possible world, where a dog can switch off a button and shrink a robot, illustrates the use of counterfactual thinking in children. They are able to problem-solve by thinking outside the box and coming up with "what could be" (see Chapter 4).

Harrison's drawing and story provide another delightful example of a kid who embodies the qualities of SPRING and GREAT – independent, organized, imaginative, and demonstrating a high level of sophisticated thinking.

Evie and Pip

Evie is aged 14 and was born in the Year of the Rabbit. Evie's mother Pip was born in the Year of the Ox.

Drawing by Evie and Pip.

Evie and Pip's explanations: "Random moments: A beautiful life"

Evie: I am the rabbit, and I'm sitting below the tree of numbers. I'm trying to work out where the number 21 is – my birthday – but I can't find it straight away. Then I try other ways of looking at it, and realize that if I add up some of the numbers which are already there – using what I have already – then I can make my own number 21.

Pip: I'm hanging by a golden rope from Evie's tree, helping her to nurture it while feeling the exhilaration of swinging from moment to moment in life. I love running around with bare feet as I don't like wearing shoes. The ox is my colorful shadow. And the black cat is the puppet master – I love cats and realized long ago that they have total control over us mere humans, it's quite humbling. The gold rope represents the golden life – so even though I'm swinging from moment to moment, experience has taught me that all of life's moments are golden. Not good or bad, just moments. The title sums up the life Evie and I live together.

Author's observations and comments

Evie and Pip crafted a story based on their animal signs. Evie, who is born in the Year of the Water Rabbit, drew herself as a beautiful rabbit sitting under a tree, which she intriguingly called "a tree of numbers." The tree bears fruit of random numbers, and Evie tried to pick out her birth date, 21 – a fascinating scenario. Unable to find the whole number 21, Evie creatively worked out how to find the number by using a combination of different numbers that added up to 21.

Pip, who is born in the Year of the Ox, drew herself swinging by a gold rope, helping Evie to nurture the tree while enjoying the freedom of being in the present moment (swinging from the tree barefoot). According to Pip, the golden rope represents every moment in life, each of which are beautiful and gold because they are precious and reflect the life she is sharing with her daughter.

Pip cleverly drew the ox as her "colorful shadow" and the cat as the "puppet master" – a nice metaphor to explain that humans who are cat lovers are controlled by the pet they are devoted to.

Evie's beautiful drawing of the rabbit showcases her artistic talent – like that of her mother, Pip, who is herself a talented illustrator. By working out different ways to find the number 21, Evie demonstrated a beginner's mind, "thinking outside the box" (see Chapter 7) and taking other perspectives, rather than being stuck in one way of looking at a situation (see Chapter 4). Pip's drawing and explanation highlight her free-spirited nature (swinging barefoot), being spiritual, helping Evie nurture the tree of numbers (see Chapter 1),and being mindful of the beauty in every unfolding moment. It is interesting to note the psychological symbolism in Pip's comments about the ox, her animal sign, being her "colorful shadow," and her love for her cat making it her "puppet master."

Overall, the compositions and stories from Evie and Pip illustrate how adults and kids can use the practice exercise to co-author a narrative together, build on each other's drawings and stories, and role-model themes from the book in a fun and entertaining way.

Lynne

Lynne was born in the Year of the Snake.

Lynne's explanation: "Mother and baby snake on change"

A baby snake asked her mother why, every few months, she shed her skin. The mother snake replied: "As I grow over time, I change physically and get too big for my old skin. So I shed it and leave it behind. But it's not just my body that changes, I am always evolving my thoughts, my feelings and how I perceive the world. Perhaps even my personality changes a bit over time. Change is healthy little snake, don't be afraid to shed your skin."

Drawing by Lynne.

Author's observations and comments

Lynne was born in the Year of the Snake. Nicholas, Lynne's son and my grandson, whose many experiences I share in this book, was also born in the Year of the Snake. Nicholas is represented as the baby snake in Lynne's narrative. Lynne's beautiful explanation of her drawing tells the story of a mother snake explaining to her baby why snakes shed their skins regularly in order to grow, evolve, and renew. Lynne was able to use the shedding of the skin – a natural, biological phenomenon – as a way of helping the baby snake (corresponding to a child) understand that everything in our bodies, minds, and personalities changes over time, and to let go when change happens. The mother snake was also able to assure the baby snake not to be fearful of change: "Change is healthy little snake, don't be afraid to shed your skin."

Being mindful, accepting transformation and change, and letting go are important and constant themes in the book. They are essential values to teach kids, but somewhat difficult to explain to young minds. Lynne's evocative drawing and profound explanation, centering around the easy-to-follow narrative based on hers and Nicholas's animal birth signs, demonstrate a unique and endearing way to teach kids deep and meaningful concepts.

Have a go and express your creativity

This chapter has provided a delightful showpiece of illustrations and stories by kids and parents that reflect the themes in this book. I am grateful to the artists for their time and effort. The beautiful drawings and explanations by kids – Acey (aged 4), Harrison (aged 6), and Evie (aged 14) – and parents Pip and Lynne show what "the artists" can come up with when they give rein to their imagination and creativity. The children's drawings are testimony to the fact that kids naturally embody the qualities of SPRING and GREAT. Their narratives also show that, with some encouragement and support from adults, kids have the capacity and intelligence to express how they would respond to the world and what they would like to teach others. This chapter also shows how adults – as Lynne and Pip demonstrated in their contributions – can use drawings and stories to express their philosophy and approach to life, and communicate complex and transformative concepts to kids.

The younger participants were not familiar with the material I was writing for my book, and the adults were familiar with only some of it. Each of them used different mediums and themes for their artwork. Nevertheless, I am gratified to discover that their drawings and stories featured and promoted universal values that are shared and practiced by many people, regardless of age, gender, and culture. All the participants informed me that they enjoyed the exercise. In fact, Acey and Harrison said they wanted to draw again!

The compositions and narratives in the chapter underline that the whole of this book is an engaging, multidimensional guidebook and primer of learning for the whole family. I hope you and your children are inspired by the drawings in this chapter to try out similar exercises, and that you enjoy letting your imagination and creativity flow freely. The insights and learnings will be invaluable for all, whether the exercises are executed by the children alone, by kids with their parents, or by parents themselves.

Chapter 20

RAISING SPRING KIDS TO BECOME GREAT KIDS

Spring kids and Great kids are like two sides of the same coin.

"Raising Spring kids to become Great kids?" you may wonder. "Isn't that a demanding task?"

"No," is my reply.

"Doesn't every parent think their kids are great?" you may ask.

"Probably," I would venture to say. But there is an important distinction between raising a Great and raising the greatest kid. In this chapter, I am not talking about the latter. I am addressing how we can raise kids to be **G**enerous, **R**espectful, **E**mpathetic, **A**ppreciative, and **T**houghtful – the attributes every parent would wish for in their kids and embodied in the acronym "GREAT".

In Chapters 1–6, you would have read about the importance I place on parents helping kids cultivate the attributes of SPRING – being spiritual, positive, resilient, imaginative, nimble, and grateful. I explain how the practice of mindfulness provides the nutrients for Spring qualities to flourish and wisdom, insight, empathy, and compassion to arise. Continuing the analogy of a spring tree, I would say that Great kids are the fruits of the tree.

How do you raise Great kids? How much effort and time do you have to put into this process? My simple answer is, "Not much." Again using the fruit tree analogy, if you put in the initial groundwork, plant the young sapling firmly in the soil, give it the right environment, and fertilize, water and care for it, the results will be beautiful fruit. There is a saying that "the apple doesn't fall far from the tree." Kids who embody the qualities of SPRING are likely to be GREAT – generous, respectful, empathetic, appreciative, and thoughtful. In my view, Spring kids and Great kids like two sides of the same coin, and the parental role-modeling I discussed extensively in Chapter 18 plays an essential role in both instances.

**SPRING kids and GREAT kids are like two
sides of the same coin.**

So what makes a Great kid? The essence of a Great kid lies in their attitude and behavior: how they respond to the world, act, and conduct themselves. Every parent, culture, and generation has a different understanding and perspective on what makes a kid great. Regardless of these differences, Great kids embody the following universal qualities.

Generous

This quality is expressed in an attitude of kindness, of giving and sharing in thoughts and in deeds, big and small. Throughout this book, I have shown numerous examples of this kind of behavior, ranging from the kindness of strangers (see the anecdote of the taxi driver in Chapter 6) or being generous to family members. In Chapter 13, I discussed how my young client Georgia generously donated the stars she earned for good behavior to her parents, sister, and dog. Georgia said: "I like being kind and giving and sharing my stars with others."

You can play a crucial role in cultivating generosity in your child in simple ways. When you share your time and play with your child, you

"I like being kind and giving and sharing my stars with others."

are role-modeling generosity. When you compliment your kids for sharing their toys with their friends or siblings, you are reinforcing their generous behavior. When you discuss with your child how they feel to have their friend share their cake, you are helping your child feel good about receiving, and consequently about sharing in return. So raising your child to embody and express generosity starts with you. It is not complicated.

Respectful

Respect is about accepting others and treating them with dignity, regardless of individual differences in values, views, and beliefs. Children learn respect when they are encouraged to act towards people with such consideration. Again, kids need positive role models from which to draw inspiration. This role-modeling can be provided by parents, family, friends, and teachers and the natural world.

While much has been written about how kids benefit from human role models, there is less discussion on how they can learn about respect from the natural world. I would like to focus on this aspect, as kids can learn this important lesson by observing the respectful ways that animals and nature engage with their environment. In Chapter 5, for example, I wrote about how the cherry blossoms flowered out of season because the tree respected the warm and wet conditions and responded by flowering profusely, and in Chapter 1 how the fallen autumn leaves respected their source by going back into the ground, nourishing the tree that gave them life.

Some people may contend that nature is just responding intuitively, and there are no exceptional lessons in their responses. This contention misses the fundamental point: that kids love to emulate behavior they observe or are curious about.

I recommend that you help your kids appreciate the positive learnings from the natural world by asking them open-ended questions and providing them with simple answers. For example:

- "Why do you think the cherry blossoms flowered so early?" "The weather has been warm and wet. Trees like that."
- "What happens to the leaves when they fall into the ground?" "The leaves provide food for the new growth."

By discussing profound insights from nature in a simple way, you are also teaching children another important lesson: that what makes their behavior respectful is not necessary actions that are evident to others, but actions motivated by their inner positive qualities.

From the human world, kids learn to be respectful when they are treated respectfully. I have discussed the various ways parents can show respect to kids through mindful communication, offering clear choices and boundaries (see Chapter 18) and allowing kids to explore solutions and possibilities (see Chapter 4). When parents behave respectfully themselves, children learn the crucial lesson that they should treat others as they would like to be treated, and respect others as they would like to be respected. Some simple examples of how you can model respectful behavior include:

- encouraging your kids to be respectful to others whether they are friends or visitors
- listening respectfully to your kids
- praising your child, not for general acts but for specific respectful behavior (for example, "It was nice when you asked me for permission to use my pen")
- owning up and apologizing to your kids when you make a mistake, so they can learn to behave similarly.

I would like to share a lighthearted and important anecdote. Some years ago, when I was invited to speak at a conference in Japan, my host introduced me to his students. The students bowed respectfully. I bowed back, and then the students bowed lower. This exchange went on for some time, with each of us bowing lower and lower in turn. My host explained that the students bowed lower than me each time because I had a higher status than them as an honored speaker and guest. I learned later that a bow in Japanese culture[40] is a nuanced form of communication expressing respect, greeting, gratitude, congratulations, or apologies, depending on the occasion. The essence of bowing transcends its physicality and symbolizes a mark of respect and appreciation.

One of the simple rules I learned is not to bow too low, as the other person would be obliged to do so as well. So the students bowing lower and lower to me was an expression of their regard for my status. It was a lovely gesture. I loved the way that a simple bow is used to express sincere and deep regard for another person.

Bowing as an expression of respect, gratitude and greeting.

Empathetic

Empathy is an important life skill for all kids to cultivate, especially when they are young. Empathy is the ability to appreciate and understand how another person is feeling or thinking (see Chapter 1). Being empathetic allows kids to feel compassion for themselves and others, and to strengthen relationships and connections. You can help your kids understand why empathy is important by asking them what they understand about this quality and how they feel when others show them empathy.

One of the most powerful ways to help kids practice being empathetic  is through activities, stories, and creative writing, where they learn to take the perspectives of others and empathize with how others might feel. For example, my daughter Lynne learned to empathize with the ants falling in the water by building a bridge for them (see Chapter 4). My grandson Matthew wrote an imaginary story about the boys who bullied Lin, empathizing with him when they were encouraged by the Buddha to understand the cause of Lin's burns (Chapter 8). And my grandson

Being empathetic is discovering how people, animals, and insects feel.

Nicholas wrote about encouraging his friends to empathize with the mosquito who bit them by understanding that the mosquito was just looking for food (Chapter 9). Similarly, you can help your child cultivate empathy by teaching them not only about how people feel but also about the feelings of animals and insects. Everything in your child's world can be used as opportunities for you to help them learn to empathize.

Appreciative

Helping kids to be appreciative is more than teaching them to say "please" and "thank you." Being appreciative is a heartfelt sense of gratitude and thankfulness. Showing appreciation also helps to reduce a child's sense of entitlement and discourage them from taking things for granted – a virtue that is worthwhile cultivating in kids (see Chapter 6). I have provided in this book many examples and simple exercises on how to support kids to show appreciation. You might like to try out the following practices with your child.

Practicing acts of appreciation

Encourage your kids to practice acts of appreciation in small ways. For example, in Chapter 14, I wrote about gifting my young client Georgia a Chinese teacup and explaining the meaning of using both hands: "When you give or receive something with both hands, it shows that you appreciate the gift." Georgia's mother informed me that Georgia employed this behavior with family members often, to show her appreciation and gratitude.

In Chinese culture, we are encouraged to give with respect and presence. When we give someone something with two hands, it is saying: "I appreciate and respect you. I am giving you my presence." And when the recipient accepts the gift with two hands, they are saying "I thank you. I acknowledge your presence. I am grateful." It is a lovely gesture of mutual regard. Next time you visit a Chinese restaurant, observe whether the waiter serves you tea with both hands. If so, you can repay the kindness by accepting and drinking the tea with both hands. This simple ritual lends itself to a feeling of reverence, care, and concern: you give the tea with care, you receive the tea with care, and you drink it with care. A wonderful gesture to teach your kids.

**When you give or receive something with
both hands, it shows you are appreciative
and grateful for the gift.**

The practice of giving and receiving with two hands is comparable to the Japanese practice of bowing, which I discuss earlier. While these expressions of respect, appreciation, and gratitude may be expressed differently in your culture, it would be meaningful for you to share them with your kids and expose them to the richness of other practices, as I did with Georgia. You can also find comparable ones in your own culture for your child to partake in.

Role-model to your kids appreciation and gratitude to people who have supported and helped make your lives comfortable. In Chapter 6, I wrote about how my meditation teacher encouraged the meditators to thank the volunteers who cooked meals at the retreat. I try to introduce a similar practice at home. For example at family gatherings, I encourage the children to try out the dishes cooked by myself and family friends, regardless of the child's personal preferences. In addition to reminding them that there are hungry kids elsewhere in the world, I add: "It is nice to appreciate the effort that has gone into the cooking, and try out every dish." Most kids I know, including fussy eaters, invariably try out every dish that is served up.

Looking on the bright side

Encourage your kids to appreciate the silver lining in unforeseen situations. If it rains on a much-anticipated occasion – for example, a birthday or soccer game – you can empathize with your kids' disappointment while pointing out something positive resulting from the situation:

"Look, the plants and lawn are happy with the rain."

"We don't have to water the garden tomorrow and we can have more playtime."

You can help your child look on the bright side and discover a possible silver lining by asking, "What do you see as something good coming out of this?"

Thoughtful

Being thoughtful is the fifth hallmark of a Great kid. It is also an important attribute of a Spring kid, as thoughtfulness is closely connected to gratitude, helpfulness, empathy, and compassion. Thoughtfulness encompasses an attitude of being mindful of what needs to be done voluntarily. I recall an experience many years ago when Jon Kabat-Zinn and I were presenting at a conference in Italy. I had been a fan of Kabat-Zinn's work, but had never met him in person. During one lunch break, I observed a man walking around the grounds mindfully collecting all the cups, plates, and rubbish, and disposing them in the respective recycling bins. I was impressed by his thoughtfulness, and only later found out his identity. I have never forgotten Kabat-Zinn's quiet acts of thoughtfulness.

Being thoughtful is good for everything and everyone.

You can promote simple acts of thoughtfulness in kids. I have highlighted many examples of such acts in this book. You can also initiate other practices; for example, encouraging your kids to help others by volunteering for community service. Model thoughtfulness yourself. When your child makes gifts for you or helps you with chores, acknowledge their kind intentions rather than just the outcomes by not being too effusive with your compliments. You can simply say, "That was very kind of you. I like how you thought of me." From these simple practices, kids will learn that being thoughtful is good for everything and everyone.

Let me return to the question and answer I put forward at the beginning of this chapter. "Is raising a Great kid a demanding task?" My answer was "No." I made the point that I was not advocating raising the greatest kid, but a Great kid. I hope that from the anecdotes, exercises and practices discussed in this chapter that you will come to appreciate that Spring and Great kids are indeed two sides of the same coin. My simple message is this: Care for your child with love and kindness like a farmer tends to a young sapling, and enjoy the beautiful fruits of mindful parenting.

Nourish the tree with love and care and
enjoy the fruits of mindful nurturing.

CONCLUSION

Spring Kids in Poetry

Poems for you to enjoy in quiet contemplation

In this concluding chapter, I summarize the themes in this book in poetry to continue the aesthetic and evocative nature of the writing and illustrations. I feel the summary can be enjoyed in a more leisurely way when expressed in poetry rather than in prose. I hope that as you contemplate the poems, they give you room to pause and offer you and your children a charming way of recapturing some of the highlights of the book.

I offer the poems in English and Chinese to showcase the meaningfulness and universal appeal of the themes across cultures. I have included here the poems about the beauty of the unfolding orchid (Chapter 1) and about being grateful to be a Spring kid (Chapter 6). The final poem, "Ode to Spring Kids," pays tribute to all Spring kids – learning to enjoy spring and reveling in the wonderful qualities of being a Spring kid. I am indebted to my Chinese tutor Kerry Wan and my friends Lydia Li and Greg Li for helping me communicate the beauty and essence of the poems in Chinese.

兰 花

The Orchid 兰 花

来, 我 们 一 起 坐 一 会 儿 吧,
Come and sit with me for a while,

我 的 唇 瓣 先 轻 轻 闭 合, 悄 无 声 息,
As first my lips are closed and sealed,

随 后 花 瓣 一 片 片 舒 展,
Then my petals unfold one by one,

微 笑 着 迎 接 阳 光 与 雨 露 的 到 来.
As I smile gently to greet the sun and rain.

起 初 我 展 现 出 一 抹 洁 白,
First I show a dash of white,

接 着 点 缀 着 几 许 棕 色 斑 点,
Then some delicate brown freckles,

最 后, 辉 煌 的 黄 色 盛 装 亮 相,
Finally my glorious show of yellow.

请 用 满 怀 爱 意 的 心 欣 赏 我,
Please enjoy me lovingly,

正 如 我 深 情 地 回 报 你 的 温 柔.
As I enjoy you lovingly in return.

Grateful 感激

作 为 一 个 春 天 的 孩 子. 我 感 谢 ...
As a Spring kid, I am grateful to ...

我 的 父 母, 感 谢 他 们 给 予 我 生 命 爱 和 仁 慈,
My parents for their gift of life, love, and kindness,

感 谢 我 的 身 心 对 我 的 照 顾,
My mind and body for taking care of me,

大 自 然 教 会 我 希 望 和 新 生,
Nature for teaching me about hope and renewal,

感 谢 阳 光, 当 我 站 在 微 风 中 时, 它 温 暖 了 我 的 脸 庞,
The sun for warming my face as I stand in the breeze,

雨 水 抚 摸 着 我 的 脸 庞, 让 我 在 它 温 柔 的 水 花 中 翩 翩 起 舞.
The rain for caressing my face as I dance in its gentle spray.

作 为 一 个 春 天 的 孩 子, 我 感 谢 ...
As a Spring kid, I am grateful to ...

我 与 万 物 紧 密 相 连,
The way I am intimately connected with everything,

我 的 父 母 和 我 的 身 体,
With my parents and my body,

与 大 自 然 阳 光 和 雨 水.
With nature, the sun, and the rain.

我 也 会 用 心 照 顾 我 的 孩 子,
I will care for my kids mindfully,

当 我 也 为 人 父 母 时.
When I too become a parent.

春天孩子们的颂歌
ODE TO SPRING KIDS

我梦想着:
I am dreaming of:

春天的颜色,
The colors of spring,

春天的香水,
The perfume of spring,

春天的承诺,
The promise of spring,

春天的成长,
The growth of spring,

春天的希望,
The hope of spring,

现在春天来了,
Now spring is here,

而我又是一个春天的孩子.
And I am a Spring kid again.

我知道,春天的孩子们
I learned that Spring kids

不受年龄,文化或种族的限制,
Are not constrained by age, culture, or race,

都能谱写属于自己的亲情故事
And can author their own love story

贝琳达 秀 鸾 康
BELINDA SIEW LUAN KHONG

当孩子们按照自己的节奏前进时.
As they journey at their own pace.

他们坚强地生活,
They are resilient in life,

巧妙地驾驭每一场冲突.
And navigate skillfully every strife.

孩子们是属灵的和积极的
They are spiritual and positive,

直观而灵敏.
Intuitive and sensitive.

他们富有想象力和敏捷性,
They are imaginative and nimble,

嘲笑生活中的每一次跌倒.
And laugh at life's every tumble.

孩子们表现出同理心和感激之情,
They show empathy and gratitude,

并且有伟大的态度,
And have a great attitude,

他们帮助年轻人和老年人,
They help the young and the old,

也表示尊重不被提醒,
Show respect without being told,

对待每个人像黄金一样.
And treat everyone like gold.

孩子们笑, 孩子们哭, 孩子们善良,
They laugh, they cry, they are kind,

孩子们的身心都很健康.
They are healthy in body and mind.

喜欢做一个春天的孩子.
I like being a Spring kid.

你为什么不试一试呢?
Why don't you give it a try?

EXPLANATORY NOTES

From a Chinese Perspective

A distinctive and popular feature of the Lunar New Year animal book series is the inclusion and explanation of the rich Chinese cultural elements and themes in the books. I continue this beautiful tradition in Raising Spring Kids. These explanatory notes contain information about:

- the meaning of the Chinese names and words
- Lunar New Year and the lunar calendar
- the Chinese zodiac – the Great Race, 12 zodiac animals and five elements
- the wood snake: general information, its personality, and famous "snakes"
- discovering your Zodiac animal sign
- the Zodiac animal sign calendar.

I hope you enjoy reading these notes.

Meaning of Chinese names and words in Raising Spring Kids

I loved choosing names for the main protagonists and animal friends in this book from Chinese terms, paying homage to my Chinese heritage, and demonstrating the elegance and meaningfulness of words across cultures. The names I have chosen also have personal significance to me and my family. With the exception of Sakura – a Japanese word for cherry blossom, which I called my imaginary friend in Chapter 5 – all the Chinese names have their origin in the Chinese language.

An important element in Chinese writing is the use of radicals. The idea of radicals is similar to the concept of root words in other languages. Radicals are pictograms (meaning "form imitation") that depict the simplest form of the Chinese character and show a basic visual representation of the word they stand for. Radicals help the reader understand the meaning, derivation, and pronunciation of each character.

The following are some of the radicals found in the Chinese names and words used in this book. I hope the explanations help you appreciate the rationale and special meaning of the words chosen.

Mulan (meaning "Magnolia")

Mulan is the name I call the little beautiful Spring girl on the book cover. To me, she symbolizes the quintessential Spring kid. Her name has special relevance to the themes of this book, and a deep connection for me.

Chinese meaning of Mulan

木　　兰

Mù　　lán

(tree)　　(orchid)

In Chinese, the word *mù*, meaning tree, comprises the radical/pictogram of a tree 木 representing growth, renewal and evolution. The word *lán*, meaning orchid, is derived from the radical/pictogram of the orchid flower 兰. Taken collectively, Mulan, the magnolia[41] – a beautiful flowering plant that is indigenous to China – expresses purity, beauty, elegance, and resilience, and holds a special place in Chinese culture and history.

Personal significance of Mulan

Mulan is also the name of the legendary female warrior in Chinese mythology who disguised herself as a man to take the place of her ailing father, a general, when he was conscripted by the emperor into the army. According to the story, Mulan saved China from the foreign invaders. The legend of Mulan was featured in the 1988 Disney movie, *Mulan*.[42] I have always loved the name Mulan and had a special affinity to it. I recalled my mother telling me that when I was a little girl, a clairvoyant told her that in one of my past lives I was Mulan, helped save China, and was a fighter for social causes and justice.

I enjoy growing magnolias in my garden. Regardless of whether I was Mulan in my past life, I am delighted to call my Spring kid Mulan and to feature magnolias on the book cover. I hope Mulan will be a good role model and help kids as her famous namesake helped China. I am sure my mother would approve.

Mei Li Chun Tian (meaning "Beautiful Springtime")

The term "beautiful springtime," which is exquisitely illustrated on the dedication page of this book, pays tribute to the memories of my mother and to the delightful Spring kids everywhere who embody renewal, growth, and hope.

Chinese meaning of beautiful springtime

美　　丽　　春　　天

Měi　　lì　　chūn　　tiān

(beautiful)　　(springtime)

The word *měi* comprises the Chinese radical/pictogram 美, representing a striking headpiece worn by a prominent person, indicating an individual who stands out. The word *lì* 丽, meaning beautiful, comprises the stroke one 一, meaning one of a kind, and the radicals 朋 which represent reindeer antlers, a symbol of beauty. Since antlers come in pairs, the radical also signifies balance or harmony.

So in Chinese, Mei-Li describes a beautiful person, one who is unique and balanced.

The word *chūn* 春 is made up of the three radicals/pictograms of grass, sun, and seed, with the sun in the center needed for the grass to grow and the seeds to sprout – all important elements announcing the arrival of spring.

The Chinese character *tiān* 天 has several meanings, including heaven, sky, season, and time. It comprises the radical/pictogram of the number one 一 and the radical, great 大 at the bottom, meaning the one great heaven or sky.

In this book, *tiān* is used to identity the different kinds of season; for example, summer (*xià tiān*), autumn (*qiū tiān*), and winter (*dong tian*).

Heaven   Great   One

Li-Kai (meaning "Beautiful Victory")

Li-Kai is the name I gave to wood snake (born in January 2025) in Chapter 17. It means "beautiful victory" and is made up of the combination of the Chinese names of my daughter Lynne (Li-Ying) and my grandson Nicholas (Kai).

Chinese meaning of Li-Kai

丽	凯
lì	kǎi
(beautiful)	(victory)

As I explained earlier, the Chinese word *lì* 丽, meaning beautiful, describes a person who is unique and balanced. *Kǎi* 凯 means victory or triumph. It comprises the radicals 山 (mountain), 己 (oneself) and 几 (several). So the name Kai represents a person who is strong and balanced; someone who can climb mountains and attain victory over many challenges in life.

In *Raising Spring Kids*, Li-Kai the wood snake, another Chinese zodiac animal, joins his animal friends water tiger, water rabbit, and wood dragon on more mindful adventures. The following are some interesting facts and information about the Lunar New Year, the zodiac animals, the Great Race, and wood snake.

Lunar New Year and the lunar calendar

In China and most Asian countries, the Lunar New Year is celebrated according to the lunar calendar, which is based on the monthly phases of the moon. The Gregorian calendar adopted in most parts of the world is based on the solar calendar and divided into 365 days and 12 months. The main difference between the two calendars is the time for celebrating certain special events. For example, the Western New Year is celebrated on the first day of the Gregorian calendar – the first day of January. The Lunar New Year is celebrated on a different date every year, usually around late January or early February, with the actual date being determined by the timing of the full moon. The Year of the Wood Snake begins on January 29, 2025 and ends on February 16, 2026.

Red – A lucky color during Lunar New Year

Red is considered a lucky (auspicious) color at Lunar New Year. Most people celebrating this event wear items of clothing with red for luck. In the Lunar New Year animal book series and in Raising Spring Kids, many of the illustrations are livened up with dashes of red to make the reading experience come alive for kids. In this book, water tiger cub, water rabbit, and wood dragon continue the tradition of gifting wood snake with a pair of red socks for luck. Small gifts of money are placed inside little red packets and handed out to younger and older family members as presents, analogous to the giving of Christmas presents These items are considered symbols of luck and help the recipient ward off any misfortune.

The Chinese zodiac

The Chinese zodiac is a traditional classification system that dates back over 2,000 years. This classification is based on the lunar calendar and a 12-year cycle, where each year is assigned to one animal. The order of the 12 animals is: Rat, Ox, Tiger, Rabbit, Dragon, Snake, Horse, Goat, Monkey, Rooster, Dog, and Pig.

This order is explained in the legend of the Great Race. According to the legend, the Jade Emperor – an important figure in Chinese mythology who is considered to be a wise, benevolent immortal – held a competition, called the Great Race for all the animals in his kingdom. Whichever animal arrived at his palace first would be accorded its place in the race.

The Chinese zodiac is further divided into the five elements of nature: metal, wood, water, fire, and earth. The five elements combine with the 12 zodiac animals to produce a 60-year cycle. For example, a wood snake (2025) occurs once every 60 years. The next wood snake will be in 2085.

The wood snake

The wood snake (2025) is the sixth animal in the 12-year zodiac cycle, following the Year of the Wood Dragon (2024), to be followed by the Year of the Fire Horse (2026). The Years of the Snake include 1941, 1953, 1965, 1977, 1989, 2001, 2013, 2025, and 2037.

The Chinese word for wood is derived from the symbol of a tree 木 (*mù*), representing growth and new life. Given the snake's intuitive wisdom and the flexible nature of wood, 2025 is seen as a year of renewal, potential, and opportunity. The capacity of some snakes to shed their skins has led these animals to be admired as symbols of personal growth and transformation. So snakes are considered in the Chinese culture to be auspicious creatures.

Chinese meaning of snake

蛇

shé

(snake)

The Chinese character for snake 蛇 comprises the worm radical 虫 and the radical 它 representing the pronoun "it", for an animal, with a roof over it. Collectively, the two radicals form the word "snake". The pictogram below shows interestingly how the worm radical has evolved in the Chinese language over the years to become the current snake word.

Evolution of the Chinese character for
the word "snake".

Personality

It is believed that a person born in the year of the zodiac animal has the personality attributed to the nature of that animal. People born in the Year of the Snake are seen as wise, calm, creative, talented, and intelligent, with a lot of aspirations. They are also regarded as charming, witty, and charismatic, with a flair for leadership. On the negative side, they are perceived as being secretive and stubborn at times, and tend to hold grudges.

Some well-known personalities born in the Year of the Snake include President Xi JinPing (water snake), Chairman Mao Zedong (water snake), President John F. Kennedy (fire snake), Stephen Hawking (gold snake), J. K. Rowling (wood snake), Taylor Swift (earth snake) and Prince George (wood snake).

Determining your zodiac animal sign

A different animal represents each Chinese Lunar New Year. The date of your birth (day, month, and year) determines your animal zodiac sign. For example, a person born between the January 29, 2025 and the February 16, 2026 is classified as a wood snake. A person born between February 17, 2026 and February 7, 2027 is classified as a fire horse.

The following illustrated table can help readers determine their zodiac sign.

Zodiac Animal Signs

rat	1948	1960	1972	1984	1996	2008	2020	2032
ox	1949	1961	1973	1985	1997	2009	2021	2033
tiger	1950	1962	1974	1986	1998	2010	2022	2034
rabbit	1951	1963	1975	1987	1999	2011	2023	2035
dragon	1952	1964	1976	1988	2000	2012	2024	2036
snake	1953	1965	1977	1989	2001	2013	2025	2037
horse	1954	1966	1978	1990	2002	2014	2026	2038
goat	1955	1967	1979	1991	2003	2015	2027	2039
monkey	1956	1968	1980	1992	2004	2016	2028	2040
rooster	1957	1969	1981	1993	2005	2017	2029	2041
dog	1958	1970	1982	1994	2006	2018	2030	2042
pig	1959	1979	1983	1995	2007	2019	2031	2043

ABOUT THE ILLUSTRATIONS

"A picture is worth a thousand words."

– Albert Einstein

When my illustrator Pip and I first conceptualized *Raising Spring Kids*, my brief to her was to allow the illustrations to engage and speak to readers visually and to make the drawings complement and reflect the Asian themes and stories in the book. I provided Pip with photographs of some of the personalities in the book. Using her deft skills as an artist and illustrator and her creative use of what I described as her "blue magic powder," Pip was able to translate the anecdotes and characters into evocative illustrations, making the narratives come alive and providing a pictorial guide for you and your child to engage with the book together. Vivid touches of red, an auspicious color in Chinese culture, are added to enrich the drawings.

It is difficult for me to nominate a preferred drawing as they are all stunning in their own special way. It would be like choosing a favorite child. I hope that the beautiful illustrations give you and your kids hours of sharing, bonding and lively discussions. I have provided some samples of this rich offering, reflecting:

- the Chinese, Japanese and Zen (*ensō*) cultural and creative influence on my writing
- pictorial representations of the characters in the book
- learnings from Matthew, Nicholas, and the animal friends
- illustrations showcasing imagination, wit, and humor.

You can read more about these sample illustrations in their respective chapters.

The Chinese Influence

The traditional Chinese and spring elements in this book are best captured in the dedication page. it is graced by a beautiful painting of my mother wearing a cheongsam (a Chinese national dress) and a delightful Spring kid wearing the iconic fluffy red socks. They are both relaxing in an elegant traditional Chinese courtyard, framed by vermilion doors, bamboo, and butterflies, and enjoying the promise of spring. The Chinese motif is further enhanced by the calligraphic writing of the theme, beautiful springtime in English and traditional Chinese (Hanyu) characters.

The teacup of gratitude (Chapter 14)
features a Chinese teacup with a
traditional blue and white motif - a
gift to one of my young clients, Georgia.

The Japanese and Zen Influence

The three illustrations featured above are inspired by *ensō*, a circular form of drawing (the Zen circle) that is a popular symbol in Zen calligraphy and art. *Ensō* is usually drawn in one fluid expressive stroke, with the circle either open or closed. An incomplete circle represents movement and openness. The empty space inside the black *ensō* stroke symbolizes a state of emptiness or "no-mind." Pip and I have adapted the principles of *ensō* to illustrate the wise sayings and advice from the animal friends to parents on raising mindful kids (Chapter 18).

My encounter with cherry blossoms (Chapter 5) with my imaginary friend Sakura, showcasing traditional Japanese yukata dresses and springtime in Japan.

Pictorial Representation of the Characters in this Book

A portrait gallery featuring the main characters in Part 1.

Sample Illustrations from my Counseling Stories

Illustration of Pip. myself and the artists in Chapter 19
enjoying the practice exercise in the studio.

My counseling session with Sheng
and his son Wen (Chapter 11).

My counseling session with Marie and
her daughter Georgia (Chapter 12).

Learnings from Matthew, Nicholas, and the Animal Friends

Matthew meditating with the animal friends (Chapter 7).

Nicholas and friends learning about the true nature of things (Chapter 9).

Illustrations Showcasing Imagination, Wit, and Humor

Nicholas' explanation of mindful and mind-full (Chapter 7).

"Fish bullying a dog."

"Nobody move! I'm looking for Matthew's missing brain!"

"Grandma is a ninja."

Matthew, Nicholas and I playing a funny internet game (Chapter 5).

The animal friends and family as positive role models (Chapter 18).

Raising Spring and
Great kids (Chapter 20).

Family writing project in Chapter 18.

NOTES

References and Recommended Readings

For readers who are interested in further reading and more information.

Introduction

1. Black, E. (2022, January 31). *Prescribing of psychiatric drugs to Australian kids on the rise*. https://www.adelaide.edu.au/newsroom
2. For the full study see: Klau, J., De Oliveira Bernardo, C., Gonzalez-Chica, D. A., Raven, M. and Jureidini, J. (2022). Trends in prescription of psychotropic medications to children and adolescents in Australian primary care from 2011 to 2018. *Australian and New Zealand Journal of Psychiatry*, *56*(11). 1477–1490. https://doi.org/10.1177/00048674211067720
3. *The Economist*. (2023, December, 7). *How to stop over-medicalising mental health*. https://www.economist.com/leaders/2023/12/07/how-to-stop-over-medicalising-mental-health
4. Khong, B. S. L. & Segall, S. (2021). Revisiting and re-envisioning mindfulness: Buddhist and contemporary perspectives. *The Humanistic Psychologist*, *49*(1), 1–218. https://doi.org/10.1037/hum0000238

Chapter 1: Spiritual

5. Rumi, J. *Two kinds of intelligence*. https://allpoetry.com/Two-Kinds-of-Intelligence
6. For further reading on Rumi's poem, see: Rumi, J. (1997). *The essential Rumi revised: New expanded edition* (B. Coleman, Trans). HarperCollins.
7. Whitaker, J. (2015, October 26). *Thich Nhat Hanh on an autumn leaf: life, death, continuation*. https://www.patheos.com/blogs/americanbuddhist/2015/10/thich-nhat-hanh-on-an-autumn-leaf-life-death-continuation.html
8. For further reading, see: Thich N. H. (2005). *The heart of understanding: Commentaries on the Prajnaparamita Heart Sutra*. Parallax Press.

Chapter 2: Positive

9. Dare to do. (2023, August 3). *Mastering happiness & success: The watermelon lesson* [Video]. YouTube. https://www.youtube.com/watch?v=W6wVU5b5nQk
10. Seligman, M. E. P. (1992). *Helplessness: On depression, development and death* (2nd ed.). W. H. Freeman & Co.
11. Khong, B. S. L. (2021). Walking with Buddha: Are we there yet? In Khong, B. S. L & Segall, S. Z. (Eds). Revisiting and re-envisioning mindfulness: Buddhist and contemporary perspectives (special double issue). *The Humanistic Psychologist*, *49*(1), 19–39. https://doi.org/10.1037/hum0000241

12. Khong, B. S. L. (2019). Dare we talk about responsibility in the same breath as rights and compassion? *The Humanistic Psychologist, 47*(1), 15–25. https://doi.org/10.1037/hum0000110

13. Yousafzai, M. (2016). *I am Malala: How one girl stood up for education and changed the world* (Young Readers ed.). Little, Brown Books for Young Readers.

Chapter 3: Resilient

14. UPI (1995, July 1). *Landslide kills 17 in Malaysia.* https://www.upi.com/ Archives/1995/06/30/Landslide-kills-17-in-Malaysia/8494804484800

15. Khong, B. S. L. (2016). "Should we tell?" Living a good life in the shadow of cancer: A personal reflection. *Hakomi Forum*, 28–29, 25–42.

16. Khong, B. S. L. (2009). Expanding the understanding of mindfulness: Seeing the tree and the forest. In B. S. L. Khong & C. J. Mruk (Eds.). Mindfulness in psychology (special issue). *The Humanistic Psychologist, 37*(2), 117–113. https://doi.org/10.1080/08873260902892006

17. Rowe, C. (2024, September, 8). Therapy is not always the answer: We must allow young Aussies to build "powerful and protective" resilience tools to tackle what life throws at them. https://www.skynews.com.au/insights-and-analysis

18. Chinese word for crisis. Retrieved July 20, 2024, from https://en.wikipedia.org/ wiki/Chinese_word_for_crisis

Chapter 4: Imaginative

19. Gopnik, A. (2010). *The philosophical baby: What children's minds tell us about truth, love, and the meaning of life.* Picador.

20. Key Differences (n. d). *Difference between nationality and citizenship.* https://keydifferences.com/difference-between-nationality-and-citizenship.html

Chapter 5: Nimble

21. Khong, B. S. L. (2019). Dare we talk about responsibility in the same breath as rights and compassion? *The Humanistic Psychologist, 47*(1), 15–25. https://doi. org/10.1037/hum0000110

22. The Prince and Princess of Wales [@KensingtonRoyal]. (2024, September 10). *A message from Catherine, The Princess of Wales.* [Video and transcript about her cancer treatment] [Post]. https://x.com/KensingtonRoyal

23. Fox. M. & Horacek, J. (2004). *Where is the Green Sheep?* Penguin.

Chapter 6: Grateful

24. First Five Years. (2020, December 22). *Teaching your child to feel gratitude.* https://www.firstfiveyears.org.au/child-development/teaching-your-child-to-feel-gratitude

25. Kabat-Zinn, J. (2024, November 28). *"As long as you are breathing …".* Facebook. Retrieved December 1, 2024 from https://fb.watch/uF40QI2Xhu

26. Kane, R. (2024, February 21). *The raisin meditation for mindful eating.* https://mindfulnessbox.com/raisin-mindfulness-exercise

27. Stendl-Rast, D. (1984). *Gratefulness, the heart of prayer: An approach to life in fullness.* Paulist Press.

Chapter 7: Cultivating a beginner's mind

28. Khong, B. S. L. (2021). Walking with Buddha: Are we there yet? In Khong, B. S. L & Segall, S. Z. (Eds). Revisiting and Re-envisioning Mindfulness: Buddhist and contemporary perspectives (special double issue). *The Humanistic Psychologist,* 49(1), 19–39. DOI: 10.1037/hum0000240

29. Bancroft, A. (1984). *The Buddhist world.* Silver Burdett Co.

30. Kabat-Zinn. J. (2018, 24 January). *Beginner's mind* [Video]. YouTube. https://www.youtube.com/watch?v=Vbok6_PgMKs

Chapter 8: Right view and right action

31. Bitesize. (n. d). *The Buddha and his teachings in Buddhism: The noble eightfold path.* Retrieved December 1, 2024, from https://www.bbc.co.uk/bitesize/guides/zr3sv9q/revision/3

Chapter 9: Being our nature

32. *The tale of the monk & the scorpion – short story.* [Video]. YouTube. https://www.youtube.com/watch?v=5fHQ0B52MLg

Chapter 10: In Dreamland

33. Zen Senzaki, N. & Reps, P. (Trans) (1940). *40. In Dreamland.* In *101 Zen stories.* David McKay Co. https://www.101zenstories.info/p/40-in-dreamland.html

34. DLTK's Sites. (n. d). *DLTK's Educational Activities: Aesop's fables: The boy who cried wolf.* https://www.dltk-teach.com/fables/boy-wolf/index.htm

Chapter 14: Empowering kids through role-modeling

35. Mind for Therapy. (2024, February 12). *Understanding systemic therapy: A comprehensive guide.* https://mindfortherapy.com/what-is-systemic-therapy-and-how-can-it-help

36. O'Brien, B. (2018, January 24). *Indra's jewel net*.
    https://www.learnreligions.com/indras-jewel-net-449827

Chapter 15: Working with challenging kids

37. Khong, B. S. L. (2013). Being a therapist: Contributions of Heidegger's philosophy
    and the Buddha's teachings to psychotherapy. *The Humanistic Psychologist*, *41*(3),
    231–246. https://doi.org/10.1080/08873267.2013.779908

Chapter 17: Am I a snake?

38. China Highlights (2024, August 23) *Year of the snake, 2025*.
    https://www.chinahighlights.com/travelguide/chinese-zodiac

Chapter 18: Tips for nurturing mindful kids

39. Grey Frames (2018, January 17). *A cup of tea: Short Zen story* [Video]. YouTube.
    https://www.youtube.com/watch?v=O-uSQvsC6x4

Chapter 20: Raising Spring kids to become Great kids

40. Sethi, S. (2024, May 27). *Why do the Japanese bow?*
    https://www.scienceabc.com/humans/why-do-the-japanese-bow.html

Explanatory notes: From a Chinese perspective

41. Chinese Showcase (2024, March 29). *Magnolia flower meaning in Chinese culture*.
    https://www.chinese-showcase.com/en-au/blogs/fengshui/magnolia-flower-meaning-
    in-chinese-culture
42. Movie Predictor. (2022, 11 March). *Mulan (1998) Movie trailer* [Video]. YouTube.
    https://www.youtube.com/watch?v=Ff80lQWbGE0

About the Author

Dr. Belinda Siew Luan Khong, PhD is an internationally distinguished Australian-Chinese psychologist, academic, researcher, and mindfulness teacher. She is a fellow of the American Psychological Association, the APS College of Counselling Psychologists, and was an adjunct fellow of Macquarie University, Sydney. She counsels individuals and families on emotional well-being, good mental health, mindful parenting, and positive flourishing. She is widely recognized as one of the leading psychologists on the integration of Western and Eastern psychologies and philosophies.

Dr. Khong is a member of the editorial board of *The Humanistic Psychologist* journal. She was the co-guest editor of a special double issue on "Revisiting and re-envisioning mindfulness" (*The Humanistic Psychologist*, APA). Her first book, *Am I a Tiger…?*, in the Lunar New Year Animal Books for kids was published in 2022. Her second book, *Water Rabbit Mindful Adventures*, was published in 2023 and her third, *Dragon & Animal Friends Mindful Adventures*, in 2024.

For more of her work, visit www.belindakhong.com

About the Illustrator

Pip Tweed is an illustrator and graphic designer. She lives in Melbourne, Australia with her daughter Evie and two cats Dora and Frankie.

Visit www. letterdot.com.au

MORE BOOKS BY THE AUTHOR

More Books by
Belinda Siew Luan Khong

www.belindakhong.com

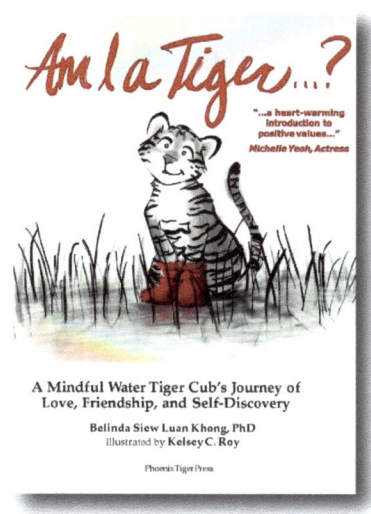

Am I a Tiger…?
A Mindful Water Tiger Cub's Journey of Love, Friendship, and Self-Discovery

After losing his stripes, a lost cub wonders if he really is a tiger after all. Join the little cub on his journey of discovery, meeting big tigers, mischievous jungle animals, and a mystical phoenix who teaches us that differences are only skin deep, and that compassion, gratitude, and friendship unite us all. The book contains explanatory notes about the Lunar New Year, and a delightful Chinese zodiac calendar for readers to discover their own zodiac signs.

"… a great book for children, parents, and families who want a heart-warming introduction to the positive values of mindfulness, gratitude, love, and compassion …"

— Michelle Yeoh, Best Actress, Academy Awards, 2023

"… a delightful tale of a tiger cub's search for love and friendship …"

— Chris Ruane, former UK Member of Parliament

"… destined to become a classic of children's literature."

— Dr. Scott D. Churchill, Professor of Psychology

"… children will open their hearts to the timeless wisdom of awareness, kindness, compassion and self-worth …"

— Janet Etty-Leal, Mindfulness Educator and Author

Water Rabbit's Mindful Adventures
The Great Race of Animal and Human Friends

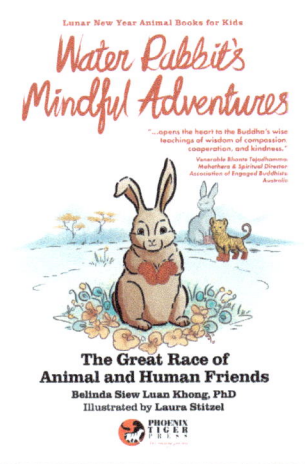

Water Rabbit's Mindful Adventures is an inspiring book filled with humorous poems and beautiful illustrations to help kids learn about mindful leadership, cooperation, communication, giving to charity, and using creative solutions to deal with conflicts and bullying. The book contains explanatory notes about the Lunar New Year, the personality of people born in the Year of the Rabbit, and a zodiac calendar to discover your Chinese zodiac animal sign.

"… opens the heart to the Buddha's wise teachings of wisdom, compassion, cooperation, and kindness."

— **Venerable Bhante Tejadhammo, Spiritual Director, Association of Engaged Buddhists.**

"A sweet and uplifting tale for children, with a heart-warming message."

— **Sue Lynn Tan, bestselling author of Daughter of the Moon Goddess**

"This book series is destined to become an exemplar in children's literature for promoting psychological wellness and competence. It is highly recommended for school, clinical and family settings."

— **Kathleen H. Dockett, EdD, Professor Emerita of Psychology, United States**

"A wonderful children's book that encourages a higher level of thinking, where the reader appreciates the benefits of collaboration through friendship, effective communication, compassion, and cooperation."

— **Neil McWhannell, Independent School Principal (retired) and former CEO, Educate Plus**

"We have enjoyed working with Nai-Nai, seeing how her dedicated work ethic is as inspiring as the characters she has created. Her book is humorous and conveys a compelling message."

— **Matthew & Nicholas D'Cruz**

Dragon and Friends' Mindful Adventures:
The Great Race Again!

Join Shan-Long, the wood dragon, and his zodiac animal friends in another great race organized by the Jade Emperor. This is a heart-warming story promoting the positive values of mindfulness, gratitude, appreciation, selflessness, teamwork, and compassion – important antidotes to many mental health issues. The book integrates the wisdom of Eastern and Western philosophies, psychologies, and the great spiritual traditions. It features exceptional animal characters, beautiful illustrations, and inspirational poetry. The twists and turns of the plot make this distinctive book a page-turner.

"I encourage anyone looking for their dragon to enter into Belinda's tale of Shan-Long, to draw encouragement and find inspiration for the great race of life itself."

— **Venerable Bhante Tejadhammo, Spiritual Director, Association of Engaged Buddhists**

"Belinda's creative tale awakens us to our own true nature and to the child in each of us."

— **Geoff Dawson, Psychologist and Zen Buddhist teacher**

"Colorful flights of the imagination, lessons on life's wisdom, folklore of the Chinese zodiac, Buddhist teachings, and animal characters that are relatable to children …"

— **Louise Sundararajan, PhD, EdD, Psychologist, and Author of Understanding Emotion in Chinese Culture (2015)**

"Practicing kindness to promote goodwill instead of gaining a competitive edge is an important moral to teach children. This along with beautiful illustrations and an interesting plot is what makes our Nai Nai's book so enjoyable to read."

— **Matthew & Nicholas D'Cruz**

"The storyline is interesting with good explanations of culture and the special friendship between animals and humans."

— **Alex Saba**

www.ingramcontent.com/pod-product-compliance
Lightning Source LLC
Chambersburg PA
CBHW040902120626
46551CB00001B/131